What readers are sayi

MW00667133

"Having served in the healthcare industry as a nurse, health advocate, and educator for 30 years, I found this to be a heart rending account of a family's struggle with a child's illness and a mother finding the heart to use her voice to save her son's life. This book is an explicit representation of a healthcare system that is broken and fragmented. It provides great meaning in a time of need for all people facing illness and confronting the challenges of navigating unfamiliar and often intimidating territory."

- Vanessa Laurella, RN, PhD
Director, Park City Medical Center, ProHealth Lab

"Mother and son's telling of Kevin's story of tragic misdiagnosis and suffering shine a spotlight on the deeply rooted problems with our medical system today, from the misdiagnosis that sent them down a path of suffering to having to pay for the very treatments that made him worse. The simple but profound message of their odyssey is *Listen*."

- Shelly Braun, PhD
Medical Anthropologist & Health Policy Analyst, Utah Health Policy Project

"This book should be given to medical students on their first day of residency. And then it should be required reading for board certification in every specialty."

- Jill Christensen
Curriculum Specialist, Park City School District

"What an amazingly horrific yet triumphant experience."

- Jeanne Peterson
Landmark Property and Realty

"I couldn't put this book down. I tried to walk away several times but had to pick it up again. I felt dread, much dread, guilt, hope, relief, fear and a roller coaster of every emotion possible. There are so many ways in which we can relate to this terrible experience. Moms, people with or people who know people with chronic, life threatening illnesses, teens; everyone can relate to this story."

- Susan Arsht
Communications Doctoral Candidate, University of New Mexico

"I see a lot of potential use for this book in nursing programs, as each student will be a future provider who needs to learn to 'listen' to his/her patients."

- Ronda Lucey, DNP, FNP-BC
Associate Professor, Westminster College School of Nursing & Health Sciences

"Riveting story... I finished it in one sitting which is quite unusual for me. This story brought many emotions, with raindrop tears, anger, happiness and fear, and other emotions I just cannot describe. I really felt like I got to know the Whiting family, which to me now represents strength. I admire their endurance through such a wicked journey."

- Linda Muir
Director, Center for Entrepreneurship, Westminster College

"I certainly didn't think a book about healthcare would be a page turner, keeping me up half the night. This is an incredible story!"

- Angie Welsh, MBA
Breast Cancer Survivor & Author of Flowering In the Desert

"As a writing duo, Kevin and his mother, Vicki, are extraordinary. They tell their story with grace and honesty. I read the book in one sitting."

- Julie Hooker
English and Leadership Teacher, Treasure Mountain Middle School

"This book arrived at the perfect time in my life; the honesty; the vulnerability… the indomitable courage and endurance. Reading it was cathartic."

- Danielle Clarke
Eighth Grade English Teacher, Seattle School District

"I had a very hard time putting this book down. Vicki and Kevin Whiting are both wonderful writers and beautifully invite the reader into their story. Their story will give many others the courage to persevere."

- Gretchen Spreitzer, PhD
Professor and Chair of Organizations and Management,
University of Michigan, Ross School of Business.

"This is a story of strength, courage and hope. At first glance the book might be categorized as a true story about a young man's life threatening illness, and a *How to Survive Guide* from a kid's perspective, but it is much more than that. It is an open, emotional, real world story about how our healthcare system and its dedicated well-intentioned members can go astray, leading to near fatal consequences."

- Kenneth Morley
Director of Operations, L-3 Communications

"This is a story about a family with infinite courage and determination, and the narrative rings true with all that is true about the resiliency of the human spirit."

- Peter Ginsberg
President, Curtis Brown Agency

"The reflection, honesty, integrity and spirit within which both Vicki and Kevin Whiting wrote will indeed be beneficial to others."

- Kathleen Campana
Mother of a Severe Burn Victim Survivor

"Refreshingly honest... Fifteen-year-old Kevin's voice is very funny, insightful and mature."

- Deena McCoullough
President, Northern Insuring Agency Inc.
Keynote Speaker for NAMI on behalf of Suicide Prevention

"Beautifully written. I love the format of the two alternating voices. I am humbled and awestruck by the sheer grit and tenaciousness of this story."

- Marcia Clouser
Board of Directors, Colorado Red Cross

"Captivating and brutally honest. It makes me reflect on my parenting and the life of ease that I take for granted."

- Carrie Thompson
Senior Vice President, Citywide Banks

We dedicate this book
to all of the Stevies, the Charlies, the Sams
and all of the other kids living in a world
of uncertainty and pain. Hold on to hope.
There are people out there who will
listen to you and make it better.

In Pain We Trust

www.vickiwhiting.com

Back cover photograph by Jill Orschel

Published by:
Blooming Twig Books LLC
PO Box 4668 #66675
New York, NY 10163-4668
www.bloomingtwig.com

ISBN 978-1-933918-88-4

First Edition, First Printing 2011

In Pain We Trust

A Conversation Between Mother and Son on Their Journey from Sickness to Health

By Kevin & Vicki Whiting, Ph.D.

Table of Contents

PROLOGUE

Dancing in the Rain

Mom

Writing this book is the hardest thing I have ever had to do. As I wrote, I relived the trauma of the story, and realized that in all probability, Kevin should be dead. But he is not. He is here to write this story with me in the hope that we can keep someone else from having to live our story.

Let's face it – 15-year-olds shouldn't be writing prologues. Of course, it is my opinion that they really shouldn't be writing books either. They should be hanging out with friends, tormenting their sisters, ogling other teens, learning to drive.

And so, when it came time to write the prologue to this book, as with so many other areas of life, the duty became mine, as *Mom*. Just like, as *Mom*, I gave Kevin his first haircut while strapped to a car seat. And just like, as his mother, I worked my way through the medical system, fighting at every step for the best care that would heal my son's fragile body.

On these pages, Kevin has written about his experiences from his perspective, detail by detail, and I have countered with my own. This is a mother's journey through the sickness of her son, and the first-person pain of the son himself. My narratives focus more on the details and the *system*, and Kevin's stories bring the emotion back into the picture.

You might find it odd that a parent would have success co-writing a book with her teenager. Trust me, when my older son

Phillip was 15, I would have found the prospect rather preposterous. But this is part of Kevin's story, as well.

Our family has always played together, allowing us to communicate and connect with one another. This tight-knit family structure helped prepare us to deal with the medical odyssey we were about to face, but falls short of qualifying for book writing synergy.

The relationship that my son and I developed as a result of his illness made it possible for us to work together on this book. The more precarious Kevin's health situation became, the more closely he relied on me to understand, support, encourage, research, advocate and manage his situation. Parents with a child suffering from a complex and/or chronic medical condition know that the parent-child relationship becomes defined by the illness. The more Kevin's illness gripped his body, I found that he became less independent than his brother was at 15, and even less independent than he had been at 13.

Our mother-son relationship became more reciprocal the further we became entwined in the healthcare system. Many in the medical community did not see this relationship as beneficial, and often took our closeness as an indication of some underlying psychosis. Nothing could have been further from the truth. In fact, it was Kevin's ability to know himself and my ability to listen to him and understand what he was trying to communicate that in the end kept Kevin alive. Kevin's voice, weak from the weight he lost week by week, silenced by the pain that tortured his body, needed assistance if it was to be heard.

Looking back on the two years our family worked through issues related to Kevin's illness, I realize that life has a way of preparing you for the next phase. Rather unlike the foreshadowing of a college professor telling his students the week before a quiz, "Listen up, students, odds are good this part of my lecture will show up on next week's quiz," life prepares you emotionally for a child's sickness in less obvious ways.

Unbeknownst to our family, life foreshadowed our future: we had the opportunity to practice our resilience during our 2004 vacation to the Oregon coast. In so many ways, it was an utter disaster. In our 2004 holiday letter I wrote:

> Our Oregon vacation, true to the 'Family Vacation' script, challenged us to look for what was right with the world. A runaway puppy, flat tires next to smelly, decaying livestock, a blown transmission, freshly broken ribs, 1,500 miles spent shuttling between broken car and family, and a total trip reroute could have resulted in 'the worst family vacation' imagined. But get this...we decided to celebrate what was right...and it worked! Strangers lent us a nearly new Tahoe to use for ten days to tow our tent trailer; travelers picked up Jeff as he hitchhiked between Bend and Burns, Oregon; animal lovers found and returned our run-away six-month-old puppy; our transmission blew with three thousand miles left on our warranty; auto mechanics worked diligently to get us back on the road so we could eventually return home; and campgrounds, hotels and friends found space for us without reservations so that we could enjoy the beach, the sand dune buggies and the Redwood forests of the West Coast. Talk about a celebration of what is right with the world! If nothing had gone wrong on the trip, we wouldn't have had the opportunity to see the 'right' that surrounds us each day.

While Kevin's illness was much harder to endure than a series of mishaps along the route of a vacation, his optimistic response to our bumbling vacation gave me insight into how he would deal with adversity. I recall how Kevin joked in his dark style about our bungled vacation in Burns, Oregon, and how the town "burned" our transmission.

Eventually he used his dark humor when he faced medical procedures that most patients could barely come to grips with. Just as he joked about our burned out transmission, during long stays in the hospital he would joke about the uncomfortable procedures he endured.

He was able to stay strong in spite of two years of unending pain, months of uncertainty, hundreds of medical procedures and the loneliness and sadness that accompany a long, hard-fought battle against an unknown medical foe. An invasive procedure that caused him to lose much needed weight, he determined, would be a great product to market to obese Americans. Kevin even bolstered our flagging spirits with the pranks he played on the medical staff during long hours trapped in the hospital. It was his idea to fill his urine sample cup with apple juice; then he dared me to take a drink of his "sample" in front of the night nurse.

Humor and pranks alone weren't enough to keep me going during the long days and lonely nights spent fighting for Kevin's life. Two dear friends who have endured their own hardships handed me pearls of wisdom that I held onto during the dark period of Kevin's sickness and recovery.

Kathleen reminded me to *keep living* as we worked to understand and cure Kevin. "This is not something that you manage your way through until you get back to a regular life," she taught me. "This *is* life."

Several weeks later, a brightly colored photograph taken by my friend Deena arrived in the mail. The sun shone through the rain onto a colorfully painted chair. The inscription on the chair in the picture read: *Dance in the Rain.*

Our family did keep living, and we are back to a "normal" life. We must keep dancing in the rain, smiling through our tears, for the journey doesn't end with a diagnosis. The journey doesn't end with a surgery. And it doesn't end with an "understanding" that the past is the past. For now, we will keep dancing through life's storm clouds.

When Kevin returned to school in the fall of what was to be his last truly healthy year after our Oregon adventure, he wrote an essay entitled “Onward to Oregon.” He captured his take on our experience with the following words:

> Unfortunately, our transmission blew out about two hours from Bend. Luckily, we were able to borrow another car. After a few days of doing fun things along the Oregon coast, we picked up our repaired Suburban and stayed one more night at a friend’s house. My dad had promised that since we had not been able to go to San Francisco, we would go to a water park instead.
>
> We had a ton of fun. Our trip could have turned out horribly, but we made the best of it and had a great time.

I would wish this type of healthcare experience and the painful re-telling of the story on no one. And yet, as Kathleen and Deena reminded me, this is the way life stretched out in front of us, and in this rainy dark chapter of our lives, we chose to dance.

CHAPTER ONE

In the Beginning, There Was Pain

(March 2007 – August 2007)

Mom

My son looked at me with pleading eyes. He clutched his stomach, held on to the plane's airsick bag, and with tears in his eyes pleaded with me, "Mom, what's making me hurt so bad?"

Thirty-thousand feet above the earth, my icy glare forced the 6-foot-8-inch tall frequent business traveler to reluctantly give up his cherished aisle seat, so I could sit next to my son. "Mom, what's making me hurt so bad?" How could I *not* sit near him?

As the tall traveler relinquished his seat for me, I fended off derisive comments from the flight attendants. I acted like a mother bear, taking care to shield her cub from attackers. The attendants barked on about boarding procedures and seating preference. I didn't care. My son needed me.

The flight was a blur of standing, reclining, praying, crying, sipping, distracting, and worrying. My fear was that whatever was causing my son so much pain would not go away as it had in the past, and he would live like this forever, or worse, that it would kill him.

He sat next to me holding his stomach, roiling with pain. What can a mother do to care for her child? There was no medicine aboard the flight that would relieve his agony. I prayed then that his ailment would go away. But we weren't so lucky. The pain had only just begun.

The weekend in Los Angeles had started off so well…

When each of our kids turn 13, I take a "Teen Trip" with them. It's a chance for us to bond before they get too old, a chance for them to be spoiled and try activities they're not used to doing at home.

They choose where we go: some exciting location for a long weekend, a stay in a hotel, fun things to do, restaurants to sample, and all the rest. Then, in their minds, when I become that overbearing Mom-of-a-teenager, somewhere in the deep recesses of their brains, they might recall that I am also human and maybe even *fun.*

Kevin's weekend in Los Angeles was an extra special Teen Trip. He was thrilled that he would be able to spend the afternoon with UCLA coaching legend John Wooden. What an opportunity for an athletic 13-year-old!

The weekend began so well. We landed in Los Angeles and then excitedly checked into our hotel. Kevin was looking forward to the chance to sit down with the coaching legend and to see the sights of L.A. But everything changed quickly: for the Teen Trip, for Kevin, and for our family.

Kevin

I thought a "Teen Trip" with Mom would be completely boring. I was having too much fun playing soccer to think about leaving my buddies on the team for a long weekend of hanging out in a city of my choosing with her. *Are you serious?*

My older brother Phillip seemed to have had a great time in San Francisco when he turned 13. He chose what they did, where they ate, and he had Mom's full attention while they rode the trolley cars and visited the Arcade Museum on the wharf.

The Teen Trip was one of Mom's crazy ideas. She loves to travel, and I think maybe this is a way for her to get to go more places. My younger sister, Katie, has been planning her Teen Trip for years, thinking about where she can swim with dolphins, go to a great beach with lots of dogs, maybe see the American Idol finales or watch some famous jazz musician. *Whatever.* I don't think there is such a city.

I suppose a Teen Trip would be a cool thing for a lot of kids. My Dad even thought the idea was so great that he got into the action, and plans a 16-year-old Teen Trip with each of us kids. As for me, I was really happy playing on my soccer team and hanging out with the guys.

Finally, when I was closer to 14 than 13, I guess my Mom convinced me that I should come with her on a Teen Trip, and even arranged the trip so that I wouldn't have to miss soccer. That, of course, was her main selling point.

Mom had this idea that our Teen Trip would give us some time together that I could look back on later, so in the back of my brain somewhere I would remember that she was a nice Mom. Once I got into my later teens and stopped remembering that she was a decent human being, that is.

Given the way that the trip and the next two years turned out, I doubt that I will hit that point most teenagers come to with their mothers, but I must admit, the Teen Trip did provide a pretty, um… different, shall we say, start to my teen experience.

I spent so much time thinking about soccer, and going to school, and all of the rest that I never got around to choosing a city for my Teen Trip. Mom asked me where I wanted to go, and I said, "San Francisco, like Phil… That's fine with me." I really didn't care that much.

I didn't want to go during the spring soccer season – it was too important to me, so we waited to take the trip until summer. Then I got what we thought was the flu, so we waited more... Then I had my wisdom teeth pulled and went to soccer camp two weeks later, anyway. *Yes, I still headed the ball, swollen cheeks and all.*

After my final soccer tournament in August, there wasn't much time left to take my Teen Trip during my *thirteens.* Mom told me that she was going to be traveling to Los Angeles with our friend Mark Eaton, a retired NBA All-Star. She was working with him on a book, and they would be interviewing the great basketball coach John Wooden, who had won more games than any other coach in all time! *Now or never,* Mom figured, and she asked me if we could combine my Teen Trip with the interview. And so we left for Los Angeles.

At that time, I never could have had any idea what kind of struggles would be ahead of me.

Mom

The weekend didn't go quite the way I had hoped, to say the least. First, there were my quiet concerns. Of my three kids, Kevin has always been the most laid back. He has a wicked sense of humor, a smile that melts the coldest of hearts, and a personality that smoothes the wrinkles that sometimes occur between the strong personalities of his older brother and younger sister.

For the past calendar year, though, Kevin had been ill an unusual number of times. Never quite sick enough to go to the doctor, he just didn't feel well, was often nauseated, didn't have much of an appetite, and increasingly lost some of the abundant energy that typically accompanies adolescent years. He tired far faster than ever before.

My internal explanation was that he had a recurring flu. The "bug" caused him to miss a good deal of school in seventh grade. Yet he advanced to eighth grade, somehow having accomplished his schoolwork while being sick.

Jeff (my husband, Kevin's Dad) and I were relieved when summer arrived, and Kevin could focus on his first love: soccer, and his reason for living: friends. His nausea, pain and fatigue came and went throughout the summer, but he didn't let them stop him from playing soccer or even from refereeing for his competitive soccer league so he could earn money to buy soccer jerseys. Sometimes I would catch the agony in his eyes; occasionally we would drive to a game with him stretched out across the back seat of the car, clutching his stomach, waiting for him to be well enough to join his friends on the field.

It was at this time that I made the only decision regarding Kevin's illness that I regret. Looking back, I had no idea how sick he was or how hard the next years were going to be. I was being pragmatic.

Jeff and I decided to have Kevin's wisdom teeth as well as four additional teeth taken out, and then, to compound his misery, we had the orthodontist slap on some braces. This was the worst decision we could have made for a child who would become increasingly ill. But how could we have known?

And did Kevin complain? No, he did not. He doesn't have a mean bone in his body, doesn't hold grudges, and according to my friend Ann, he has no lessons to learn, but instead lessons to teach *us.* Let me explain. Ann told me about the theory that, if you believe in reincarnation, a person comes back to earth to learn lessons they missed in earlier lives. She is convinced that Kevin has no lessons to learn, and has no reason to be back here on earth except to teach *us.* Based on the way he responded to recurrent flu-like symptoms, braces, pain, life on feeding tubes, stomach pumps, and Peripherally Inserted Central Catheter (PICC) lines, I believe her.

Yes, absolutely, I feel guilty thinking back on the pain that we inadvertently heaped on our son in his time of trauma, with the tooth pulling and all of the rest. Guilt is a horrible reality of caretakers and of survivors. And, it's not helpful when parents are in the deep dark tunnel of keeping their child alive.

And so we travelled to Los Angeles, Kevin and I, for his Teen Trip. We met my friend Mark Eaton and his son Doug for a portion of the journey. Thank heavens we did. Two teenagers sitting side by side, the football linebacker next to the soccer mid-fielder provided a stark contrast. It began to dawn on me that Kevin's body was more "frail" than "naturally thin."

During that trip I noticed how little Kevin was able to eat in a single sitting compared to Doug. I noticed how each of Kevin's ribs was clearly visible with each in- and exhale of his chest when we headed down to sit in the hot tub at night.

And worst of all, I began to notice how Kevin's pain was interfering with his everyday life. Instead of goofing around the par three golf course in his normal playful manner, Kevin humored me and agreed to play only after a bit of cajoling.

My son didn't even want to go to the beach. When I finally talked him into the 10-minute drive from our hotel, he jumped twice from the sandbank, listened to the roar of the crashing waves for a few minutes, and then asked if we could go back to the hotel to rest.

Perhaps I had been living with subconscious denial, ignoring each of Kevin's episodes of not feeling well, not noticing his gradually thinning frame. Our Teen Trip allowed me a chance to finally notice that something was really wrong with Kevin. But still I was in denial, and I was not anywhere near prepared for the trials to come.

Kevin

The weekend started fine. We rented a convertible so when we picked up Mark and his son, Doug, up at the airport the next morning, there would be room for Mark's tall body to stretch out.

The hotel we checked into was *way* fancy. The only problem was I really couldn't eat. I'd been having trouble eating for a while. Nothing sounded good, and I felt bad most of the time. So I'd eat weird food: pancakes, smoothies, maybe some Rice Krispies.

Instead of checking out the beach or going out to eat when we got into Los Angeles, I just wanted go to the grocery store, grab some cereal, and hang out in the hotel room and watch movies. Since it was *my* Teen Trip, my mom stayed in the room with me, and that is exactly what we did.

The meeting the next afternoon with Coach Wooden really should have been the most amazing time ever. He is the nicest guy in the world. Instead of telling us all about how he got his guys to win all of these games (he was the "Winningest Coach in History"), he wanted to know about *us.*

He did tell us stories about his wife, his kids, and his grandkids. He told stories of his early days, when *his* coaches had helped him be a good player and coach.

It was *crazy* to sit in this condo full of every award a person could possibly get. He had a Medal of Freedom from the President of the United States, and his own picture on a Wheaties box, and huge crystal basketballs from winning the college championships so many times.

And, instead of telling us how great he was, *Coach* (that's what everyone calls him) wanted to spend time talking to Doug and me about how we should do our best at whatever we decided to do. He told us over and over that we *were* winners as long as we gave something our best effort.

Coach told us to be strong and to work with other people. Not in a lecture kind of way, you know, *"Oh I know everything because I'm so successful,"* kind of way, but in a grandfatherly, *"I want you to have a good life,"* nice way.

I wanted to be able to really listen to what he was saying, especially because he was so nice, and because Mom and Mark had told Doug and me how much Coach had done for the world. They told me how Coach had worked hard so that black players could play in college tournaments, and how he had been so involved in the Special Olympics.

It was amazing that I got to be there in Coach's home because he had made a difference for so many people who hadn't believed they would ever be anything… but I felt awful. Really awful. The sickness that had been coming and going all year was getting really bad.

Finally, when I couldn't stand it anymore, I took my Mom to the side and told her I thought I was going to throw up. Mom stays pretty calm at times like this. We couldn't leave, she said.

Mom knew I was sick, so she showed me where the bathroom was, put her hand on my forehead, hugged me, got me as settled down as she could, then she went back to the interview.

I went to the bathroom, and she finished the interview, and we made it through somehow. We gave it our best effort.

Mom

Even now and then I become melancholy as I think back on how hard Kevin tried to make the weekend special for us. We met Mark Eaton and his son Doug at LAX airport and the four of us prepared to head out to Encino to talk about mentoring with Coach Wooden.

What a sight we were. The top on the PT Cruiser was down to accommodate Mark's tall frame. Next to 7-foot-4-inch tall Mark, Kevin was so slight. His weight (unbeknownst to us) was hovering in the low 70s at a time when his buddies were bragging about hitting the 100-pound mark. His weight was far below the 90-pound minimum healthy weight for someone his height.

The weather had predicted rain. In the spirit of adventure (and to make room for Mark's head), we drove with the top down, ducking in and out of rain clouds on our way to meet the legendary coach. As Doug tried to talk us into putting the top back up, to avoid the occasional raindrop, Kevin remained unusually quiet in the backseat.

We stopped for lunch at Pancho's. Still quiet, Kevin ate nothing. I coaxed a few bites of cheese into him, knowing he had only had pancakes for breakfast. I was worried, but there was nothing terribly out of the ordinary. I still thought he was fighting a lingering flu.

We finally made it to Coach Wooden's residence, Kevin looking pale and still quiet. But he knew the significance of the meeting, so Kevin remained strong. He asked questions and took Coach's pledge.

Even as he was taking in the magnificence of the experience, it was clear that all was not right. And finally Kevin broke. He touched my hand, and when we were able to break away, he let me know that he was feeling awful.

I was torn. Cutting short our visit was not an option, particularly since Kevin had no apparent acute illness – no burning fever, no unstoppable vomiting. But something was clearly wrong.

As we returned to the convertible following our time with Coach Wooden, Kevin was getting worse. Now having spent uninterrupted time with Kevin, I was sensing the scope of the problem. This was no simple flu. I was very worried.

Kevin was having trouble eating, and he was painfully thin. He didn't complain, but he was often in pain. I wanted to get him home right away and start to figure out how to make my son healthy again – so we headed to the airport for an earlier flight.

Once at the airport, a bomb threat had turned security lines into temporary rest stops. No one was moving anywhere. I gave up all hope of getting home and began devising alternative plans.

Out of nowhere, however, a security guard asked Kevin and me to follow him to a separate entrance. We were admitted to our concourse along with the Cincinnati soccer team. A professional soccer team! Imagine! Kevin's dream-come-true.

As I engaged the team in conversation while we cleared security and waited for boarding instructions, Kevin gave up even trying to talk to the players. That troubled me more than anything else. When Kevin won't talk to professional soccer players, he must be in serious trouble.

Staying as calm as possible, I assessed the options: an hour and a half flight, local doctors, family and support, or stay in Los Angeles, get immediate care, relief for Kevin's distress, and potential life saving medical intervention. He had no fever, no chills, but rather a severe version of his on-going pain and nausea. We would take this flight.

Just before the doors closed we stepped on board the flight and took the last two available seats. Just as we were sitting down

Kevin looked me in the eyes and told me I *had* to sit next to him. I sat down near him, looked into his pained eyes, and I knew our nightmare had begun.

I recall that flight with great agony. I felt as if the journey would never end. I had no idea it was only a prelude to the symphony of horrors to come. Looking back, I would have done anything to help Kevin bear the pain. In the moment, however, I am proud of how I responded. I am glad that I stood up for my son's needs. I am relieved, in hindsight, that I was brave enough to get on the plane and listen to my instinct that said it would be better to be ill at home than in a strange city.

That Teen Trip was a wakeup call for me. My son needed me, and I needed to be there with him. During that meeting with Coach Wooden, all of our lives changed forever. And now, my only focus was to seek help and health for my son.

Kevin

Coach Wooden told us that day to do our best, to be strong. His words would become my constant refrain over the next months and years of my life. When I was at his home, I took his pledge.

Coach Wooden's Sportsmanship Pledge

Success is happiness in your heart because you made the effort, 100% to do your best.

I'll be a good sport
When I win or I lose.
No whining, complaining
Or making excuse.

I'll always keep trying,
One hundred percent
To give my best effort,
In every event.

This sportsmanship pledge
Will bring out my best.
Coach Wooden has taught me
To be a success.

Of course, the things that he said that day help basketball players win lots of games. I mean, obviously they do, right? His teams won all their games. But to me, it wasn't about winning games anymore – it was about how I needed to be strong if I was ever going to get rid of this pain and be a normal kid again.

Coach taught me about doing my best and finding people who will listen to me, and about how we need to listen to other people, especially if we need help. And how people need to work together to get through a hard game or hard times.

A lot of the things that he said that day stayed with me as I got sicker and sicker. I would remember what he said to me, or Mom would remind me what he said, and I would stay strong for one more day. Or I would do my best to do what the doctors asked me to do. Or I would find someone who would really listen to me.

And day after day, I started to understand what it was that Coach was really talking about. And I stayed strong.

CHAPTER TWO

Ouch, Ugh, Yuck

(September 2007)

Kevin

It must be bad.

Both of my doctors were there to take a look at me. As soon as we got home from Los Angeles, Dad met Mom and me at our family doctors' office. Dr. Rush and Dr. Dolan have been seeing everyone in our family for over 10 years.

I have no idea what Mom said to Dad, but I knew my parents were scared because they were never *both* with me at an appointment. Usually Dad was busy getting his business running, and Mom would take me to my appointments when she's not teaching.

The first thing the doctors did was to give me a shot that made me feel better than I had for a long time. Then both doctors pushed on my stomach, asked me a bunch of questions, and mixed up this really gross medicine that I had to drink.

I had hardly been to the doctor except for my school shots since I had an earache when I was four years old, and I didn't swallow medicine. I wouldn't take pills or antibiotics or even vitamins. Any weird taste or a pill to swallow would make me gag.

Now the doctors mixed up this gross looking concoction in a little mixing cup and four adults stood in front of me waiting for me to drink it.

I looked at the puke-pink drink and thought that maybe I'd rather just stay sick. Weird thoughts ran through my mind.

I thought about the television show *Fear Factor* and how I could never compete on that show because contestants had to swallow all that gross stuff. Maybe I could try out for *Survivor*, instead. Those contestants didn't have to eat, and their lives seemed miserable. I was getting really good training for S*urvivor*.

I could tell that everyone was getting really frustrated with me, even though they were trying to act like they weren't. It was miserable. After what seemed like forever I swallowed down the medicine, and I almost threw it back up. Finally, I was able to keep it down, and we went home.

I wasn't all better, but at least my parents were convinced that whatever was wrong with me, I could be at home, and I didn't need to go to the hospital. At least not yet.

Mom

Of the four adults facing Kevin late in the evening in our family doctors' office, perhaps I was the only one who understood the magnitude of the challenge in front of Kevin.

Kevin had not, could not, would not take medicine.

After his dental surgery he chose not to take pain medication, including ibuprofen, due to the severe gag response any medication caused him. Prior to his dental surgery we bought several tubes of mini-M&M's thinking that Kevin could practice taking the M&M's just in case he ended up with an infection and had no choice but to take the antibiotics. In the end the M&M's proved such a challenge that we decided to take a wait and see approach – if Kevin needed antibiotics to ward off an infection, he would figure out how to drink the liquid or swallow the pills.

And here we were, in this room, four adults staring at Kevin, hoping that he could swallow this strange concoction called a *GI Cocktail*, made up of liquid Benadryl, Lidocaine and Pepto-Bismol, all stirred into a two ounce plastic medicine cup, ready for Kevin to consume.

No doubt this revolting mix of medicines would taste as bad as it looked. As Kevin steeled himself to chug down the mixture, I caught my first glimpse of the determination that would carry Kevin through the upcoming battle. Down went the medicine, followed by several swallows as it threatened to come back up, followed by walks around the office to keep it down.

When I called the doctors' office and explained what happened in California, they said to bring Kevin right in. They would stay late to see what could be done. How fortunate we were to have an established relationship with our family doctors. They were willing to take my call from the plane as we touched down. Both doctors worked together, trying to understand what was wrong with Kevin. They listened to all I had to say. They considered Kevin's symptoms in light of their long history with our family.

One look at Kevin's condition, and the doctors prepared a shot of morphine. As the medicine quickly dulled his senses, the relief from pain allowed Kevin a chance to relax and explain with a bit more coherence how he was feeling.

Doctors Dolan and Rush listened carefully, pushed and prodded on Kevin's abdomen and determined that Kevin was in no acute medical danger. Clearly, they agreed, he was in real agony, which perhaps, they thought, stemmed from gastritis. They assured us that gastritis can be incredibly painful, symptoms can come and go, and if left untreated, the pain will get worse over time.

The first plan of treatment was to keep feeding Kevin the GI Cocktail to relieve the pain and soothe his upper GI tract. In this way Kevin's body could heal. Uncertain how Kevin was going to keep taking the gross pink goo, Jeff and I shared a look that confirmed we would figure out a way.

With the help of the morphine and the GI Cocktail, Kevin finally felt well enough to get some liquid into his body – the first that actually stayed down in over 24 hours. This was a routine that would prove to be effective. If Kevin got into dire straits because he couldn't take in enough liquid and nutrition, the doctors would provide him the medicine he needed to mask his symptoms. Then he could take in life sustaining liquids and nutrition.

Over the next few weeks the severity and frequency of Kevin's symptoms increased at an alarming rate. The intent of the GI Cocktail was to allow Kevin's GI tract to heal, if there was indeed gastritis causing the severe pain. The ghastly drink would theoretically also relieve the symptoms so that he could eat and drink while his body healed.

In truth, Kevin could barely eat and drink without feeling nauseous and later writhing in pain. Jeff and I quit worrying about homework, soccer practice and family meals. We spent each evening camped out beside Kevin watching fearfully as even sips of Gatorade became hard for him to consume. Kevin's only source of nutrition became slowly sipped protein smoothies. Kevin was wasting away in front of our eyes.

The lack of response to this treatment suggested that Kevin was not suffering from gastritis. There were, however, many other *-itises* that could cause the type of focal pain Kevin was experiencing – the kind that made it impossible for him to eat, drink, study, read, play, or laugh. As the complexity of his pain and the lack of response to standard medicines grew, our family doctors recommended that we have Kevin seen by a pediatric gastroenterologist.

We made calls to the specialists recommended. Not one of the specialists had time in their booked schedule to see Kevin. The earliest appointment we were able to schedule with any GI doctor was six months out. Many of these specialists were no longer admitting new patients. Kevin could not wait six months. Finally, with the backing of our family doctors and Jeff's persistence, we found a compassionate doctor who agreed to have Kevin come into his office during his lunch hour.

Before we were able to make the appointment that was two weeks out, Kevin was struck by a particularly horrific, painful episode. Frightened by the intensity of his pain, worried by the lack of fluids Kevin was able to take in, watching him throw up the pink, gooey medicine he forced down in the hope it would ease his pain, I called our family doctors once again.

"Get him to the Emergency Room," they told us. "He's not responding to the medicine, this could be serious. More tests should be done." Kevin was losing weight, and his pain was increasing.

As we rushed Kevin to the hospital, I called my parents.

"We're heading to the Emergency Room," I said. They had stayed in close contact since Kevin's pain episodes had become so significant. "The doctors want to rule out appendicitis."

Perhaps Kevin had appendicitis, perhaps the appendix had ruptured. I was afraid; this meant surgery.

"We'll be there if you need our help. You're all in our prayers." My folks were always the first people to get in their car and drive wherever they felt they could help.

Jeff sped to the Emergency Room, Kevin's body doubled over in pain, his head resting in my lap. I tried to soothe the pain with a gentle back rub, soft strokes to his forehead. During the drive we talked about what our doctors had told us, and why this might be appendicitis. The appendix isn't always located in the lower right quadrant; sometimes it is located in a different part of the abdomen. Even though his pain was upper left, maybe he was just put together a little differently. We tried to convince ourselves that an appendectomy wouldn't be such a bad thing, especially if it cured Kevin's pain.

The pain worsened. Jeff drove faster, afraid Kevin's appendix would burst. We had to get him to the hospital before the infection spread throughout his body.

Kevin

The medicine didn't help me. Over the next weeks I would go back and forth between the doctors and home. I would sometimes get a shot to take away the horrible pain, and I would get different medicines to try. Then I would go home and try to eat some kind of food. I'd try not to throw up the medicine or the food I had eaten.

Every once in a while I would make it to school for a class or two, but mostly I would lie in pain and drink Gatorade. This was when I named my pain.

There was one place in my stomach that hurt so bad I can't even describe it still today. The pain was always the same place, and it was just miserable. I don't know why I decided to name my pain, but suddenly one day the name *Burnie* popped into my head because it felt like I was burning up from the inside out.

I could put two fingers on the worst part of the pain, and it never moved. My family doctors said that there was something important about the fact that my pain never moved and that I always put my fingers on the same place.

Finally, one day the pain was so bad, the gross pink medicine wasn't doing any good, and I was feeling worse and worse. My family doctors said we had to get to the Emergency Room to look and see what was really going on inside my body. So we went to the hospital.

I don't remember the first trip to the Emergency Room as being really bad, but I remember looking over at Dad during one test. He looked like he was going to pass out. Probably, now that I think about it, what they were doing to me did seem gross. They stuck a big tube in a private part of my body and filled me up with water or something so they could get good pictures of my stomach and all of my guts. If I was healthy and they did that to me, I think I'd pass out like it looked like my dad was about to. It might even mess with my head for the rest of my life. But since I was in so much pain, well that's probably a clue about how bad *Burnie* was. Seriously, it was awful.

Nurses know this. When a nurse would put in an IV, or give me a shot, and I would just hand over my arm or tell which vein was best, the nurse would get a real sad look. She knew that this meant that I had spent *way* too much time with *Burnie.*

But that first time I went to the Emergency Room, I didn't care what they did to me, no matter how painful, as long as there was a chance of making *Burnie* go away.

At Primary Children's Medical Center, the people doing the procedures worked hard to make a bad thing not so bad. This helped me handle the stuff they did to me. And I had already been feeling so bad for so long, that if it meant that I would start to feel better, then I was willing to be strong and go through whatever I had to so I could feel normal again.

The people at the hospital took my mind off what was going on by finding things to talk to me about. They gave me nice things to smell, or music to listen to. And I liked the way they told me why they had to do certain things to me. They would explain exactly what was about to happen.

I feel bad that other people go through the gross procedures that I have, because really, they are not nice. But if a kid has to go through them, I hope they can have them done at a place like Primary Children's Medical Center where it seems like the staff will try anything to make bad procedures as good as possible.

Mom

Kevin was pale from pain, weak from dehydration, and lethargic from weeks of nausea and lack of adequate nutrition. We were afraid that his appendix might burst or had already. Surely in this weakened, pain-wracked state, he would be seen ahead of the rest of the children, toddlers and infants crowding the hospital's Emergency Room.

I looked around me at the room full of worried parents: several mothers holding coughing, feverish babies, parents trying to settle a toddler hopping around on one foot, the other ankle swollen, a child hugging his painful arm to his chest. Beside me sat an aunt, explaining that her niece had been ready for the family portrait when her brother pushed her. "She hit her head on the edge of a table. I think she needs stitches." More children arrived, and Kevin languished.

Minutes turned slowly into hours as Jeff and I tried unsuccessfully to engage Kevin in cell phone games to distract him from his pain. The crowded Emergency Room waiting area felt like a prison while we waited our turn to see the physicians and machines that would help Kevin.

As each child was called for check-in, my frustration grew. I wondered how the child that had a 102 fever beat Kevin's pain in the triage filter that determined which child should be seen first. Selfishly, I judged the parents waiting with me, making assumptions about which illnesses and injuries should be seen by regular doctors. *They should not be using the Emergency Room doctor as their personal family physician*, I thought to myself.

By the time Kevin's name was called he had fallen into a restless sleep, still refusing to drink any of the Gatorade Jeff had bought for him in the cafeteria. Once in the examining room,

Kevin had to be weighed.

The numbers that flashed up on the LED screen meant nothing to me. His weight had dropped down into the mid-60s, so some type of alarm should have sounded in my brain. Looking back at pictures taken of Kevin during this phase of his life, I had failed to notice how painfully thin he had become. Instead, I was focused on the pain that was keeping him from eating.

Not everyone was focused on Kevin's pain, however. His low weight became the central focus for the parade of doctors who were soon to enter our lives.

Emergency room physicians confirmed what our family doctors had been telling us. There was nothing urgently wrong with Kevin. No appendix was about to burst; no kidney was soon to fail. All of Kevin's organs looked fine on the ultra sound, and there was no mass or blockage in his lower intestines.

However, the ER doctors did think that checking Kevin into the hospital would help him. First, Kevin could get some much-needed nutrition. Also, pain medication could be continued so that Kevin could have a longer break from the pain that had consumed his life. Finally, and most important of all, the doctor attending to us in the Emergency Room explained, checking Kevin into the hospital would give us access to a broader range of diagnostic testing in a shorter period of time.

We were looking for the most direct route to get Kevin well, so we agreed with the Emergency Room doctor's recommendation to check Kevin into the hospital and get additional tests started.

As the double doors that separated the Emergency Room from the rest of the hospital swung open, the attentive Emergency Room physician made a reasonable request that would soon vibrate through my head during our dark hospital stays:

"When you find out what's wrong with Kevin, would you let me know?" she asked. "Juvenile gastro [abdominal] problems are so tough to diagnose. The causes are evasive, the tests are invasive, and the symptoms are sporadic. We're seeing more and more cases like his, and I'm never sure what diagnostics I should perform here in the ER to understand what's wrong with all these kids."

Up on Pod Q of the hospital, Kevin was assigned to a tiny, dark room tucked into the end of a quiet corridor. With no clear instructions from the Emergency Room, no gastro-specialist assigned to Kevin's case, and a hospital crew that appeared to be overwhelmed by the sheer number of patients who needed to be admitted, I felt as if Kevin was imposing on the serious medical problems other patients were facing.

It was clear that the team assigned to care for Kevin were unsure as to what procedures should be ordered in an effort to diagnose what was causing Kevin's pain. I knew that his pain was the primary problem. I felt that if we could solve the pain, my son would once again eat, be active, and regain his energy and muscle mass.

One thing did become clear; the medical team was very concerned about Kevin's weight, and rightly so – Kevin's weight to height ratio no longer registered on the curves that track healthy percentages for kids. During this first hospital visit, an overworked attending doctor wrote in Kevin's chart that he appeared *anorexic.* The doctor used this word as a short hand description of Kevin's lack of appetite.

Once we passed through the ER and were ushered into this new domain where specialists knew best, a few doctors who scarcely knew Kevin and his story came to a dangerous conclusion based on this shorthand medical note. They read his *anorexic* lack of appetite as *anorexia,* which is a psychological diagnosis, not an observation of physical symptoms.

With no clear lab result, X-Ray, CT scan or condition, the doctors had no foundation to declare, "Here is the cause of Kevin's pain." And so we were left with conjecture. We were sent home after a short hospital stay with directions on how to "Power Pack" – to cram as many calories into each bite Kevin consumed. The goal was to increase his body mass. He was also given more prescriptions for stronger anti-acids with hopes that these would calm Kevin's pain. Our appointment with the gastro-intestinal specialist was coming up. Until then, our job was to fill Kevin up with as many calories as possible.

We placed a white board with columns in Kevin's room. One had the time of day. The next was labeled "food / drink." The third column identified the number of calories associated with food or drink. Finally there was a column for Kevin's medicine and another to track his weight. Each day, every time Kevin swallowed, we tracked how many calories he consumed or what medicine he took.

We waited for the corresponding increase in his weight that would accompany his new "power-packing" diet. Unfortunately, the more peanut-butter/butter/maple syrup covered waffles Kevin consumed, the greater his pain became. Each milkshake, made with half and half, rich creamy ice cream and whole milk made Kevin feel nauseated. So, while tracking his elusive yet expected weight increase on the white board, I began to track other items in the day planner I carried with me everywhere I went.

Three times a day I would touch base with Kevin and ask about his appetite, his pain, and his energy. Unbeknownst to Jeff, Kevin or any of his doctors, I created my own tracking measurement based on what I felt were important symptoms to understand. I called my measurement Kevin's "APE" score. I looked for patterns in Kevin's appetite, pain, and energy levels, searching for clues. Reviewing Kevin's "APE" results, I became aware that a short while after eating, Kevin's pain became intense, his appetite would disappear and his energy would become depleted.

Kevin was better in the morning. He woke up feeling fairly well, often able to go to his first class. He was often okay until he consumed a corndog as part of his school lunch, if he hadn't had too big a breakfast. Kevin would force himself to eat, though often he could only swallow a few bites before his body rebelled.

The records I kept told me that Kevin was willing to try to eat what the nutritionists from the hospital said would make him better. He would force down what he could, but this food did not have a nourishing effect on him. Just the opposite. The more food he forced in, the greater his pain, and the lower his appetite and energy.

This was just the beginning. At least during the first trip to the Emergency Room, the tests did not show appendicitis. I had my moment of relief. But then reality set in.

No one knew what was wrong with my child.

CHAPTER THREE

Horses and Zebras

(October 2007)

Mom

Prior to a second, longer hospital stay, Jeff had been able to get Kevin seen by one of the few gastro-intestinal specialists willing to take on a new case. At the appointment the doctor was alarmed by Kevin's symptoms. Due to Kevin's low weight and the significant amount of pain he endured, this specialist scheduled Kevin for an Upper-GI procedure the very next day. The procedure would be done on an outpatient basis and would rule out all kinds of issues, the specialist assured us.

At the hospital the next day, Kevin was put under general anesthesia so a camera that snaked down his esophagus, through is stomach and into his intestine, would allow the doctor to get a look at Kevin's throat, stomach and upper intestines. He was tested for Celiac Disease, Crohn's Disease and ulcers.

Calling us that night, the doctor informed us that there was evidence that Kevin's stomach was in distress, but there was not enough evidence to explain the significant level of visceral pain of which Kevin complained. Still, there were new medicines to try. He prescribed drugs that would coat Kevin's "fried stomach, covered with *Petechiae* (red spots resulting from tiny ruptures of blood vessels under the stomach lining)" along with other, stronger anti-acids that would neutralize his stomach acids. He suggested certain dietary restrictions to determine if perhaps there was an allergy or food intolerance causing Kevin's illness.

Still, Kevin's weight plummeted. Following up in the doctor's office the next week, the specialist felt Kevin's condition was fragile enough that hospitalization was necessary in order to stabilize Kevin's weight and manage his pain. With relief, we learned that in the hospital an entire team of specialists would be assigned to Kevin's case. The more minds, the quicker the answer, we reasoned. Once in the hospital though, Kevin's condition was predetermined to be anorexia, as had been suggested in the medical notes from Kevin's first hospital record, where the doctor had written *anorexic* for his lack of appetite.

"You are asking me to look for zebras," the doctor informed me, using an insider-physician analogy for how Kevin's diagnosis would be handled. His somewhat standard diagnosis of anorexia for Kevin's weight loss (a *horse*) pre-empted a serious look for any less likely explanation (a *zebra*). This made no sense. He continued, "When you hear hooves you should look for horses." I couldn't believe my ears.

Having been admitted into the hospital a second time, we had already spent over a week at Kevin's side. He was connected to a jangled nightmare of IV tubes delivering pain-relieving medicine and a nasal-jejunal tube threaded up his nose to provide nutrition. There were heart rate monitor pads attached to his chest and an oxygen saturation bandage wrapped around his toe. A team of doctors made morning rounds scratching their heads and looking for clues. A variety of psychiatrists, psychologists, and social workers held daily interviews to determine Kevin's mental health.

Kevin, trying to take in nutrition in spite of his pain, explained again and again how he was feeling. Kevin described what his life was like outside of the hospital. Kevin clung desperately to my hand 24 hours a day as teams of doctors, nurses and hospital staff moved in and out of his room. This constituted Kevin's hospital experience. No answers came forth, no relief from the burning pain occurred.

During the long, lonely nights, alarms sounded as Kevin's heart rate steadily decreased, as his weight decreased, as his pain increased. The nurses lowered the point at which the alarm would sound, until the machine was set to sound below 40 beats per minute. That was the limit; fewer than 40 beats per minute, Kevin would need to be checked. Yet the alarm kept sounding, and Kevin's heart rate continued to decline.

Yet every morning the doctors arrived with no answers to the source of Kevin's pain, and then they stopped recommending tests that might help determine what was wrong. And so I started asking questions. They had run out of their "horses" and I kept begging them to find the "zebras".

There was no diagnosis to fix what was wrong with Kevin, and there did not even seem to be any relief for Kevin's pain. As my son's body shrank smaller in his hospital bed, so did his spirit. But mine did not. The hunt for zebras would continue.

Kevin

Did you know that you can turn your body into a fountain? Or that if a tube isn't put through your nose into your stomach the right way, it could get tangled in your vocal chords? How about the fact that nurses help you put different items (like tootsie rolls and nickels) in lab samples as jokes if you are in the hospital long enough?

Yeah, well, I wish I didn't know any of this, but I ended up learning all of this stuff and a bunch more when I got put into the hospital the second time.

The first time I was in the hospital wasn't too bad. I was there for only a couple of days. I got my pain kind of under control, they took some pictures of my stomach, and drew a bunch of my blood. But mostly they talked to me about how I should be eating a bunch of high calorie food. Did they think I didn't want to eat all the food my friends ate?

That first time in the hospital, my Dad's business partner came to see me. He knew all the cool things to do in the hospital since his wife worked there. A couple of my friends even stopped by and we fooled around with the bed's controls, and we played the Playstation games the hospital had, and then we watched the movies they let patients check out.

The second time I went into the hospital sucked big time. I was in awful pain most of the time. I had really thought that by going to the hospital, I would finally start to feel better.

My brother, sister, and I loved to watch the TV show *Scrubs.* I guess maybe, when I thought about going to the hospital, I figured I'd have cool doctors like JD and Elliot who would come around and get to know me and get me well quick. Then I'd even be able to catch the last few games of my soccer team's season. But that's not what happened. Not by a long shot.

After a week in the hospital, when Phillip would stop by to see me he'd just say, "Dude, we have got to get *House* to take a look at you." *House* is a different show that my brother Phillip likes. *House*, the doctor the show is named after, is able to solve the really hard cases that no other doctors can figure out.

Nearly my entire second visit to the hospital was horrible. The only thing that made it bearable was that the nurses were really awesome. They tried so hard to help me out. And someone from my family was always right there with me, which is the only way I could stand to be in the hospital. A lot of the stuff that happened in the hospital that second visit kind of lives in my brain like a horror movie.

A horror movie for me would be set in a place where people had to drink Ensure to stay alive. I was forced to drink Ensure. Then when I couldn't eat enough food to help me gain weight, the doctor ordered a feeding tube put down my nose. Nurses fed me Ensure through my feeding tube. So the horror movie would definitely have Ensure.

Next, there would be a scene where the hero is held down while a feeding tube doesn't quite make it down where it is supposed to go. I know that for lots of people getting a feeding tube isn't a big deal. I know a couple of kids who put their own feeding tubes back in if they are accidentally pulled out. But mine went the wrong way and curled up in my throat.

The climax of the horror movie would come when the hero is told maybe these tiny little specks of grain in his intestines might be causing the problem. The evil doctor hooks the hero's feeding tube up to a special cleanser and pumps the tube full of some special liquid to "clean out the pipes." Too soon the hero's body is so full of the liquid that the liquid is spurting out of his body everywhere, like some crazy cartoon.

The evil doctor is nowhere to be found since this special torture process is only done late at night in the dark hallways of the hospital. To the rescue comes the hero's mother, who screams at the doctor's assistant and makes the assistant turn off the torture device. The doctor's assistant says he can't do anything until the doctor returns a call and approves the canceling of the cleansing procedure.

A good ending for the horror movie would be the evil doctor coming into the hospital room and seeing the pain and suffering he had caused the hero, for no reason at all.

The other part of the horror movie would have all kinds of people showing up every afternoon to grill the patient. Each afternoon psychologists or some kind of person who wanted to ask me questions would come in and ask my Mom to go get some coffee while they talked to me alone. It wasn't usually the same person, but the questions seemed to be read from the same script.

The crazy thing is that the psychologists or their assistants seemed to know what answer they wanted me to tell them, so they kept asking me the same questions. Maybe these doctors hoped I'd tell them the answers they wanted to hear.

First the psychologists would ask me about school. I kind of got the idea that being a good student wasn't such a good thing to them. They would make it seem like Mom and Dad *made* me do well in school, which is totally wrong, but I just answered their questions. I really didn't want to talk very much because I felt so lousy; I just gave them answers to whatever they asked.

Next, the social workers or whoever was doing my daily grilling would ask me about soccer, but not how much I liked it. I love soccer more than anything. These hospital workers wanted to know how good I was and how much I practiced and how much my team won. Maybe I would have talked to them about some of the teams I really like and my favorite players, but it didn't seem like that was what the script called for. The interrogators just wanted to know about how hard I worked as a referee and how many games I would play and how much time I played in each game so I just answered those questions too.

Then the interrogations got really weird. The staff would ask in a way that made me think that they knew something I didn't. "Had I been bullied?" I hadn't. But I don't think they liked that answer. And they wanted to know if I had been raped. I hadn't. I think they believed me, but they kept asking anyway for the next eight months.

One time the question asker let me know that if I was confused about my sexuality I should feel comfortable talking to her about it. When I told her I would feel more comfortable talking to my mom about all of this stuff, well, she really didn't seem to like that at all.

I'm writing this like I was really good at talking to these psychologists, but I wasn't. I was terrible. I'd mumble one or two words or just nod my head. See, I was in terrible pain and I was trying to deal with it, and I thought their questions were stupid.

It's hard to talk when I'm in pain, so a lot of times I would ask my Mom to answer the doctors' questions for me. She had been with me all the time for months, and I had explained to her how I felt. She had seen me go through my pain, and when I heard her explain things, she answered just like I would. Most of all, I really trusted my Mom and she was right there so when they would make her leave I would get pissed. So a big part of the horror movie would be the interrogation part.

There would be good parts of the movie too. You know how in these movies there are good parts to lull you into thinking everything is going to be okay? That happened in the hospital too.

Sometime during the day I'd have pain medicines that helped me forget about my pain, I didn't have to eat, and there were no doctors around. Maybe some friends would come by to hang out, or maybe my grandparents would stop by when my brother and sister were in school. My dad would come by and we'd play some cards or something after he got done with work.

But a lot of what I remember were late nights, watching all of the *Scrubs* and *Office* episodes, and lots of movies with my mom. I had to have my mom with me every night. We'd figure out jokes we could play with nurses we had become friends with. Mom would make a chart of how I was feeling and how different medicines made me feel. Most of all we'd try to figure out why I hurt so bad.

Mom

"You are asking me to look for zebras." In retrospect, the doctor's faulty logic was clear. Kevin's problem was not a horse, it was not even a zebra; it was a black rhinoceros from sub-Saharan Africa. Oh how I wish I had questioned his faulty logic. What kept me from speaking up against his false analogy?

Maybe it was my exhaustion. Ten nights propped up next to Kevin's hospital bed, hospital noises and worry had made me sleep deprived and unable to think to ask what this doctor meant about horses and zebras. Perhaps the doctor-patient power relationship and my belief that this was his area of training kept me quiet. He was a triple-board-certified pediatrician and psychiatrist; he must know his horses from his zebras. As I struggled to meet all of the demands placed on me, I no longer had the energy to question the logic behind his argument.

I tried to balance Phillip's high school educational demands, Katie's middle school emotional demands, and my unavoidable work commitments with Kevin's medical demands. Whatever the reason, I lamely bought into the doctor's logic. I charted Kevin's pain, and his response to medicines. Late at night I visited the National Institute of Health's website to better understand Kevin's symptoms and his responses to the anti-depressant and anti-anxiety medicines he was taking.

I was right there, all day, every day. I could see Kevin's health declining. Unfortunately, as my child lay suffering, I was too overwhelmed by the multitude of demands placed on me and not well enough informed to make my voice heard. The unimaginable stress and the weight of uncertainty made it impossible for me to recognize the faulty rationale that was driving my son's healthcare plan in the wrong direction.

Each day spent, each procedure given, each interview with a mental health professional brought Kevin further from the goal we all shared – to keep Kevin alive. After months of experience, and ample coaching from other physicians, I finally, a step at a time, learned how to become Kevin's medical advocate. If I had spoken up, and if his physicians had truly listened to me, we could all have saved Kevin a year of uncertainty and months of suffering, let alone tens of thousands of dollars in unnecessary tests and treatments.

As Kevin's hospital visit continued, our days took on an uneasy routine. Each morning a group of physicians and nurses would huddle at the foot of Kevin's bed. I don't remember much of these visits. I was tired and blurry eyed from a night of broken, restless sleep. I would try to follow the brief discussion of what tests or treatments the day held in store for Kevin. I tried to comprehend the most recent thoughts regarding his tenuous health status. The jargon was garbled – certain words I was familiar with, "anorexia" and "cycle of pain". Other words were scary and unfamiliar, "nasal-gastro tube" and a "go-lightly" procedure. What was clear at each of these morning meetings was the lack of consensus as to what was causing Kevin's pain or even agreement on how to determine a diagnostic finding.

Sometimes I would offer my opinion to the doctors. By tracking Kevin's medicine, I realized that the only medicine giving Kevin real relief was an anti-spasm medicine. I told the team that Valium affected Kevin in terrible ways, zoning him out, turning him into a zombie. The team of doctors looked at me, nodded their heads, but did nothing with the information I provided.

Jeff became worried about the continuous use of narcotics to control Kevin's pain. I relayed his concerns to the early morning team of doctors. They assured us that because Kevin was caught in a cycle of pain, he would not become addicted to the strong narcotics. But these medicines weren't stopping his pain. They weren't helping him get well. With narcotics in his system, Kevin could eat. He could sleep. But the drugs also slowed his digestion down and lowered his heart rate. Though we worried, the use of narcotics seemed necessary for Kevin to regain body weight although they wouldn't cure him.

After the morning meeting, I would hurry to get some breakfast from the cafeteria, to buy coffee for myself and for the nurses if they were coffee drinkers, all before Kevin woke up and worried why I wasn't by his side. From my early interactions at the hospital, I decided that the nurses would be my best allies in Kevin's cause. They took the time to get to know him; they searched for ways to ease his pain. If I could provide a bit of coffee or hot chocolate to cheer up their days, I was pleased to be able to support their efforts.

Once they knew that Kevin was willing to laugh when he

could, and would use his humor if engaged, they brought on the dry wit and trickery. Hours of watching *Scrubs* would result in playing matching games between actual doctors and actors on the show. But the nurses couldn't provide the answer we were searching for, and they were often the very individuals that had to inflict painful or humiliating procedures on Kevin. The staff personnel took the time necessary to know Kevin and what he needed from them. They did not always succeed, but they were not afraid to try.

Late one night, a nurse noticed that Kevin had failed to pee in the necessary amount of time. Hospital rules prescribed a catheter at this point for the patient's well being. No one, especially a teenaged boy, could possibly want a catheter inserted into them so that they could pee. Nurses know this better than anyone.

With doctor's orders looming in their hands and their faces long with regret, the nurses struggled to find different options. Finally, they turned to each other and mentioned a name. A call was made to a nurse with lots of experience. This angel of a nurse came into Kevin's room and played the old sleepover trick of soaking strategic parts of the body in warm water to encourage urination. Carefully, respectfully and at the same time a bit playfully, she got Kevin to loosen up and avoid the dreaded catheter.

That combination of experience, improvisation, leniency, and gallows humor helped Kevin avoid one more horrific procedure.

The dreaded announcement that visiting hours were over came at nine p.m. every night. This was the worst part of every day for our family during each of Kevin's hospital visits.

Evenings were the best part of the day. Phillip, having had his driver's license for two and half months, would wait for Katie to get home from school, and together they would make the 45-minute drive to the hospital. Sometimes they would bring along their homework, or perhaps a new game to play with Kevin on the PlayStation in the hospital room.

Jeff would drive over from his work, and we would be together as a family. I might take Katie for a walk while the boys hung out together, or Phil and I might grab money and load up on cafeteria food while Jeff and Katie played cards with Kevin. The evenings were the best part of our hospital routine.

And each night, the dreaded announcement would interfere with our time together. Jeff would have his overnight bag packed, ready to spend a night with Kevin in the hospital. We would explain to Kevin that this was the night that Dad got to stay with him while I went home to spend time with Katie and Phillip. The plan would be set, Katie bright with the anticipation of having me at home to tuck her in at night and fix her breakfast in the morning. But Kevin couldn't face the night without me. Jeff would be crushed, as he wanted so badly to be there for Kevin. Kate would break down crying, she wanted her family to be together. And another dark night of sadness, loneliness, and uncertainty would begin.

We did what we could to bring reminders of home into Kevin's airy hospital room. I suppose this was our attempt to make Kevin more comfortable in the sterile hospital environment. Kevin's hospital room had a beautiful view of the mountains. We kept the blinds open to allow in the bright sunshine. When it became clear that Kevin would be in for a longer-term hospital stay, my parents took posters off of Kevin's bedroom walls and brought them down to decorate his hospital room. Jeff stopped by the local soccer store and tried to brighten Kevin's day with an AC Milan soccer scarf to drape across the cabinet. Coach Wooden's pledge card was propped up next to Kevin's bedside along with a stuffed bear that had journeyed from my grandma to my mom to my aunt as they each worked through various health issues. Each additional day in the hospital brought more decoration until every spare bit of wall was covered with reminders of home.

No amount of decoration, bright windows or nice views could take away the fact that this was a hospital room, however. The blood pressure pump clasped Kevin's arm and squeezed tight at regular intervals. Wires attached Kevin to a heart rate and blood oxygen monitor. Tubes eventually snaked through his nose down into his intestines and stents allowed for easy access of medicines and blood draws. Decorations would never offset the medicinal smell so distinctive to a hospital setting.

Humor and optimism began to be exhausted by what felt like a constant grilling by mental health professionals. For the first days, these meetings seemed benign enough. Family history was recorded; Kevin's medical history was taken for what seemed like the hundredth time. At first I would stay by Kevin's side as he dealt with his pain and gave short answers to the questions so often answered before. At times Kevin would give me, the "Will you explain this to them?" look that we shared. And I would know that Kevin couldn't or wouldn't go into the details again, so I would summarize for the interviewer what he had said so many times before.

Eventually, the mental health team worked with Kevin alone. I thought this was good. The plan was to give him some visualization techniques, some ways to distract himself from the pain. He needed to learn these techniques if his pain was not going to go away. When the mental health team came to the room I would head over to the coffee shop, while Kevin sadly watched me leave his side.

Not all of the focus was on relaxation techniques and pain-coping mechanisms during these sessions, though. One time I returned to the room to find Kevin upset. Kevin was crying. When the hardest pain hit Kevin, he would curl up in a ball. His face would betray the visceral pain inside, but he would not cry. This crying came from an emotional place, a different type of pain. He wanted to know what he was supposed to tell these people. "What did they want to hear?" he asked. I didn't understand.

To Kevin, the mental health sessions had become "fishing expeditions" rather than "seeking to understand and teach mental relaxation technique" sessions. In frustration, he cried, "If I just tell them I was bullied will they leave me alone?" And then I began to understand. Kevin sensed the frustration that everyone was feeling – there was no answer to his pain. And he knew long before anyone else that his doctors, mental health professionals and nutritionists were not headed in the right direction.

Rather than fighting it, he wanted to know if he should just give them the answers they wanted: *that he was depressed and anxious, which caused him to be unhappy with himself, and in this state of low self-esteem, he caused his body to refuse food, and/or creating a mental cycle of pain.* It would be a logical explanation even though it wasn't the truth. But he continued to tell them what he actually felt, not what they wanted to hear.

The pain was focal, our family doctors told us, and focal pain meant he was experiencing *real* pain. More frustrating to me, however, was the fact that the horses the doctors were seeing – those of anxiety and depression – were not Kevin's reality. Yes, the longer he lived in constant pain and uncertainty, the more anxious he was. The anxiety was a result of the pain, however, not the cause.

When I tried to explain this to the doctors, I became part of the problem they were identifying. The mental health specialists said that Kevin had failed to "individuate" from me and this was adding to the anxiety and depression that fueled his ongoing pain and weight loss.

Wracked with pain, losing more weight every day, Kevin's job was to fight to stay alive, to stay strong. I made it my job to advocate for Kevin.

And I did. For months on end, for more than a year, Kevin and I did not separate for more than a few hours at a time. I could speak his thoughts and explain his needs when he was too weak, in too much pain, or when he had given up. Few people understood the fact that Kevin was not weak because of my advocacy, just the opposite. Because I was there, Kevin could be strong.

If I had been under less stress I might have taken time during the long, sleepless nights to think about how lucky we were. We had healthcare coverage through my work. We did not have to choose whether we should mortgage our house, cash in our retirement or give up on the kids' college fund in a desperate hope to find a cure for Kevin's pain. We did not have the additional stress of punching a clock, leaving Kevin alone in his bed day after day to fend his way through the healthcare procedures alone.

My job as a college professor affords a certain amount of flexibility. I was able to take a lighter teaching load in order to pursue research, so that, despite weeks in the hospital and countless days spent traveling from one doctor to the next, I was able to keep my job by working on my laptop from Kevin's bedside.

Taking time away from work was not an option for Jeff. As a small business owner, no one could do his work when he took time away to attend to the increased family demands that accompany a healthcare crisis, and Jeff had no affordable healthcare options for our family.

We were caught in a healthcare system that demanded my full time attention to Kevin's health fight while at the same time demanding I fulfill my full time job commitments. Eventually, we would learn that the system trapped us into thousands of dollars of charges incurred at the hospital that would not be covered by our healthcare plan. The healthcare benefit that would, thankfully, pay for Kevin's expensive diagnostics, hospital room and medicines, did not cover the psychiatrist bills nor charges from social workers. There were co-pays and deductibles. There were other services provided in the hospital, with no prior notice that we would be paying the exorbitant charges. We would pay these charges whether we asked for the service or not, whether the procedures were successful or not, whether they made our son better or made him worse. Our savings were quickly depleted and we had to secure a loan to offset the out-of-pocket expenses that inevitably accompany any complex medical condition.

As the bills mounted, we felt caught in the middle of a game we didn't understand. The rules of this medical game kept changing.

We were familiar with the guidelines that governed our care at our family doctors' office, but a different system of regulations determined how we were treated and the type of care we received at the hospital. A team of doctors who didn't know us, our backgrounds, or the history of this case were struggling to put together a plan of action to rid Kevin of his pain while our family doctors weren't welcome at the hospital.

Ultimately, Jeff and I realized that we were the only players in the crazy medical system game that served as a link between the enormous numbers of players involved in diagnosing Kevin. Unfortunately, at this point in the game, rather than learning what rules were in force, Jeff and I trusted a faulty system.

At times, late at night when the hospital walls would collapse in around me, I would sit on my window-seat bed, look out over the city and think maybe I was wrong. Maybe Kevin was anxious and depressed, caught in a cycle of pain due to the unintentional stress brought on by Jeff's and my wanting the best for him. Had I somehow indicated to him that he wasn't good enough just the way he was? Had I somehow made him feel inadequate? Had I missed a traumatic event in his life – a time where someone else had hurt him, or made him feel worthless? Had I somehow mistaken his witty, easygoing nature – could he be using this as a mask for some underlying fear, uncertainty or self-loathing? Jeff seemed more convinced of this explanation than I. Maybe the mental health specialists were right, and I was looking for a clue inside of Kevin that didn't exist. In these dark moments I searched the deepest memories, relived conversations and came to the conclusion that Kevin was simply a well-adjusted kid in pain. I needed to continue to listen to what he was saying. I needed to remind myself of our family doctor's statement: "focal pain is real pain." I needed to continue to research every symptom and every medicine I could find to get him well.

My parents' arrival at the hospital bolstered my belief that Kevin's pain was real. Entering the hospital room after driving through the night to come and help us out, my parents looked at Kevin and their eyes filled with tears. Jeff and I had become familiar with the sight of Kevin doubled over in pain, his increasingly frail body swamped by the hospital bed. We were used to climbing beside him in his hospital bed to place a hand on his painful stomach as he doubled himself over our warm touch. We knew that gently rubbing his back, encouraging him to breathe easily, guiding his brain to the smells, sounds and feel of his beloved soccer field would allow him to work through the pain until a new dose of medicine would overcome his senses.

For my parents the sight was terrifying. They had been spending time with some of their other grandchildren, all about Kevin's age. Kevin's condition contrasted starkly to the grandkids they had just visited.

I assumed that once the hospital team of specialists began taking care of Kevin, we were in the right hands. Our family doctors figured that since they didn't hear from us, Kevin was getting better. Nothing could be further from the truth.

Everyone in a hospital needs an advocate, and I was Kevin's. It was hard to live at the hospital, but nothing could tear me away from easing his pain and suffering, his fear and uncertainty. I wanted to be the one who was there fighting for Kevin. Always, that is, except one Saturday morning.

Convinced of the slight possibility that tiny specks barely visible on Kevin's intestinal X-Rays could be causing him all of his pain, an on-call doctor suggested that Jeff and I approve a "golightly" procedure for late Friday night. By this point in Kevin's hospital stay a feeding tube had been inserted and was providing Kevin his nutrition. The on-call doctor explained that since Kevin already had a feeding tube placed below his stomach the procedure would be quite easy.

Instead of putting the normal Total Parenteral Nutrition (TPN) into the feeding tube, super-duper laxatives would be fed through the line. Given Kevin's inability to consume regular food, the laxative should work quickly to cleanse out the granular specks, specks that appeared no larger than the head of a pin on the X-Ray. This, we were told, would rule out these dots as the cause of his pain. "He's lucky," noted the GI doctor, "With his feeding tube he won't have to force himself to drink the solution. This will be much easier on him."

Go-lightly procedures are scheduled to begin as soon as visiting hours are complete. And so, at nine o'clock Jeff left the hospital with Katie and Phil. Kevin's feeding tube line was switched from nutrition to cleansing solution. The pump that determines how quickly fluids flow into the system was cranked up. Soon, Kevin's system was feeling the effects. Cloaked in a flimsy hospital gown with his thin back end exposed to the world, Kevin rushed to the toilet, as fast as possible with the IV stand trailing beside him. He clung to my hand, as the first round of liquids most certainly cleaned him out completely, making pumping any more liquid into him futile. Soon he was throwing up the laxative, it came draining out of his nose.

Pale and terrified, he pleaded with me to call the nurses to slow down the rate at which the "go-lightly" was entering his system. I didn't dare leave his side, so I pushed the nurse call button on the wall. Quickly a nurse responded, looked at Kevin and agreed that we needed to get a doctor to make adjustments. He placed the urgent call to the doctor on-call. Late at night the only response we received to his "non-urgent" request resulted in a message back to us: indeed, the nurse could slow the rate at which the fluid was entering Kevin's intestines. However, slowing down the rate would extend the procedure from six hours to eight. Did we really want to extend the procedure?

"Slow it down." I demanded. "And get that doctor to this room." It could have been minutes, but it felt like hours before the intern appeared at the door.

"Turn it off." I declared.

"It's not run its full course." the doctor replied.

I was cradling Kevin's head in my lap, sitting on the bathroom floor. Kevin no longer made an attempt to get to the toilet. The fluid flowing from his body looked the same as the medicine being pumped in.

"Look," I said, "what is coming out is exactly the same as what is going in. What could be left that can be cleansed? His problems are low weight and pain, and this is exacerbating both!"

"*Turn it off*," I said with a mother's firm conviction.

And he did. First, he claimed that he needed to get permission from the on-call doctor that had prescribed the procedure.

"*No*," I shouted. "*Turn the pump off, or I will.*"

When Jeff arrived at the hospital early the next morning, he saw that both Kevin and I were enraged. The little nutrition Kevin had been receiving had been turned off for the torture and he was robbed of his strength and his dignity. I felt as if I had failed Kevin in allowing the procedure to take place. Kevin was given medicine to sleep, and to create a level of amnesia, distancing him from the horrific night. I was left with haunting, vivid memories.

While Kevin slept, Jeff gently stroked Kevin's hair. I told Jeff I had to get away from the hospital for awhile. Phil's high school homecoming dance was that night. I used the fact that he had no dress clothes as a reason to get away from the hospital and out into normal society for a few hours.

But even my escape was ruined.

Before I left, doctors noted that Kevin's weight was down to 63 pounds. Kevin's GI specialist found out about the procedure Kevin had been put through and was furious. How could another doctor put a patient with such dangerously low weight through such a procedure? Why hadn't he been contacted? Jeff and I had approved the procedure because the on-call doctor made it seem like a reasonable procedure that might help Kevin get well. Now, with the additional guilt of approving the procedure weighing heavy on my soul, I really needed to get out of there.

Finally out of the hospital room, I could let my emotions escape. While crying and trembling from exhaustion, I drove to a nearby clothing store.

I couldn't remember Phillip's pant size, nor could I forget the horror of the night spent with Kevin. My mind was locked on the mental image of my dreadfully thin son as I had left him, dried tracks of tears on his sallow cheeks, restlessly sleeping. I hoped he wasn't dreaming of last night, but instead had been able to conjure up memories of happier times.

My mind was a million miles away when a former student called out to me.

"Dr. Whiting, where have you been? I keep stopping by your office so that I can talk to you about the paper I wrote last semester. You are never there."

"Yeah," I admitted: "My son is horribly ill, the doctors can't figure out what is wrong. He's in the hospital and getting worse."

"Really?" Here came the dreaded question, "What's wrong with him?"

"Nobody knows. He's in horrific pain and keeps losing more and more weight. We've been trying to figure out what's wrong for two months now. He's lost over 25 pounds."

"Well, don't you worry. He's in God's hands."

Tears formed in my eyes. "Don't worry!?!" I fed back to him. "How am I supposed to not worry when every day he loses more weight, he suffers from incredible pain, and no doctor even knows what tests should be run to figure out what's wrong with him?"

"Well, everything happens for a reason. You just need to trust in God."

To myself, I thought, *What kind of God would choose this type of torture for an innocent, young child?*

In my exhaustion I wanted to scream, “You smug know-it-all. How dare you tell me there is a reason that my sweet child has spent the past months writhing in uncontrollable pain…that there is a *purpose* for him spending his days at a hospital with needles, tubes, and medicines commanding his uncertain future?”

But, as his former teacher, I offered the young man this advice instead. “You know, sometimes when people are suffering and in real bad pain, the very best thing you can say to them is: ‘I’m sorry you’re having to go through this.’”

Looking back on the exchange, I realize that he was offering words that he felt would be encouraging. But oh how they stabbed at my heart.

I wanted to trust God at that moment, but what I needed to do was trust Kevin’s pain. Kevin’s pain told us to get him out of the hospital. Far from the hopes we held when checking Kevin into the hospital – hopes of improving Kevin’s health and understanding what was wrong with him, Kevin was worse off physically, emotionally, and mentally after his long hospital stay. There was nothing being done for him there that I couldn’t provide for him at home.

And so I trusted his pain. “Focal pain is real pain,” our family doctors had said.

Before we could attack the pain, though, Kevin needed to gain weight, and he needed to recover from the emotional trauma of his continued pain and the on-going lack of a diagnosis. He needed nutrition and a safe, secure place where we could plan our next move.

And so we sprung him from the hospital.

CHAPTER FOUR

Can't and Hate

(November 2007-December 2007)

Mom

Hopelessness. I'd never felt hopelessness before.

I'd seen this look in the faces of friends. At times, I worked to alleviate it from the lives of the less fortunate. But never had I truly felt hopeless like this.

As we checked Kevin out of the hospital, with no diagnosis for his pain, I glanced at him in the rear-view mirror of my car. He had a feeding tube snaking through his nose, dropping like a fishing line into his GI tract, and I felt hopeless.

They sent us home with handfuls of prescriptions: anti-spasm, anti-depressant, anti-anxiety, anti-acid and anti-pain. We were lost in pills. We had been knocked off center. It was as if our son was a prisoner of war in a foreign camp and we didn't know whether to mourn or fight for his freedom. There was no closure. We had no way to help our son. No one seemed to have a way to help our son. We felt hopeless.

Kevin

Journal Entry – November 2, 2007

> I'm so confused. Why does it hurt so much when I'm not even anxious? I'm really getting sick of forcing my way through the pain. Almost every morning I don't want to get out of bed. I don't want to face the pain; I just want to lie in bed and cry. Is life really worth living?

There were lots of nights when I wished that I could just go to sleep and not wake up the next day. It seemed like that would be so much easier for everyone.

There was one night especially that I can remember. I had come home from the hospital the second time. I had the feeding tube shoved up my nose, and I was taking like ten pills a day. They weren't helping at all. Nothing was.

Dad had to help me walk out to the end of the driveway and back. Worse, now I was tired, too. Mom brought in an old telephone book. I tore pages out five at a time and ripped each page into hundreds of bits of paper. The pages were the pain that was tearing me up inside. I tried to fight back, but I couldn't any longer.

I couldn't even think well enough to be able to shoot at aliens or bad guys on my video games. That took too much concentration, and I couldn't even think about anything but how much my life sucked, and how it wasn't fair and how long this had been going on and how no one knew what was going on and how it was never going to change and how I was going to have to live like this forever.

There's no other way to say it. My life sucked.

I knew that all of my friends had finished soccer season without me. Every day they got to go to school and hang out together. They all went trick-or-treating. They went to the Halloween dance.

I just laid there in pain all day, and when I could walk, I had a pole that I dragged around next to me with a bag full of Ensure hanging off of it.

I didn't know what my friends were talking about anymore or who they were hanging out with, and I didn't even care. I didn't care about anything.

Mom

Perhaps my hopelessness was contagious. I met with my older son Phillip's high school teachers to ask what needed to be done to bring his sinking grades up. Although the reports of him sleeping through classes, not turning in homework, and suffering from a high number of unexcused absences reflected a completely different student than Phillip had normally been, the news did not surprise or alarm me.

How could Phillip possibly focus on school when he had spent the last weeks regularly visiting his brother in the hospital? And even now that Kevin was home, Phil worried about him, looked after his 12-year-old sister, had little parental supervision and attention, and felt that no end of the crisis was in sight. And how could I help the high school administration to understand our situation when I had no foundation myself? We did not know the nature of the beast we were fighting against, and we spent all of our energy struggling against this unknown and unseen foe. Harnessing the power to discuss our family's situation was impossible. Finding the time to meet with Phillip's teachers to explain his emotional needs was next to impossible.

I summoned the energy to e-mail the administrators at Phillip's school, asking the vice-principal or counselor to explain our family situation to Phillip's teachers. As a result of this communication, some teachers worked compassionately with him and established individual schedules that accommodated the multiple demands Phillip was facing.

But other teachers adhered stringently to the district's policies, one going so far as to explain that she was "offering Phillip a chance to understand the harsh realities of life" through her unwavering adherence to deadlines and expectations during this difficult time for him. Perhaps I was biased on Phillip's behalf, because I could not understand how such steely pessimism and callousness from a high school educator would help Phillip understand the harsh realities of life any more than our current living situation already was.

One of the classes Phillip was failing had been his favorite subject in former years. He usually excelled in this area. The message from the high school administration did nothing to alter class expectations from this particular teacher. I tried my best to reiterate the distracting home life surrounding Phillip by contacting the teacher directly. I hoped to set up a meeting where Phillip's situation could be discussed. I wanted to know what we could do to support his learning. *Perhaps we could hire a tutor*, I thought, *or maybe there were study sessions he could attend.*

No response. Finally, I left Kevin in the care of my parents and I rushed to meet Phillip as soon as school let out. We hurried to catch his teacher during the 15-minute period she had reserved to meet with parents before her coaching duties took precedence. Clearly she was not prepared to discuss Phillip's classroom problems when we chased her down at the school gymnasium.

"Can we meet at a better time?" I asked. "Phillip's brother has just been released from the hospital. He's living on a feeding tube. It's really hard for me to get away."

"This is a tough time of year for me what with the team to coach and everything," she responded.

"Maybe all he needs is a tutor, or some additional support to help him out."

I was silenced by the teacher's explanation that Phil had, "not yet crossed over the bridge between concrete learning and logic and critical thinking. He's not ready to succeed in class," she continued.

Apparently her mind was already made up as to Phillip's ability to succeed.

"Fine." I said, "In that case I need to know how to take him out of your class. How do I do this?"

The teacher appeared upset by my response. She changed her tone and said, "Maybe we should look at the situation after you have a chance to think about this."

Exasperated, I explained that we had a family crisis going on at home. It was clear to me that she was not going to work to support Phillip's learning needs, and I doubted his ability to be successful when the teacher had already labeled him as not possessing the skills necessary to succeed.

"Don't worry," I said, "I'll figure out a different way for Phillip to get his requirements completed."

As Phil and I turned to leave the gym, the teacher reached out to give me a hug. She asked if my ill son was okay. Wouldn't I reconsider Phillip's enrollment in class?

Phillip caught the irony of the situation. As I fought the tears brought on by my fury, his words turned my reaction into hysterical laughter. "And I'm the one lacking logic and critical thinking skills?" he said. "Why would your son have been in the hospital and living on a feeding tube if he was okay? Since when do they put kids who are okay in the hospital?"

Katie was struggling in a completely different way. Several times a week I would receive calls from her at her middle school. "My stomach hurts," she would sob. Or tearfully, "Will you be home tonight? I need you." These tearful calls cut straight to my heart. Did her stomach hurt in sympathy for Kevin? Was she really ill? I had to disappoint her again and again when Kevin was in the hospital, and that was heartbreaking. With Kevin's health so urgent, I knew, no matter how much I wanted to be home, that I would ultimately wind up staying at Kevin's side, sleeping next to Kevin. Katie was being robbed of my attention.

As Katie struggled to make it through her classes each day without breaking down in tears, we discovered support. Her team of teachers and counselors not only took care of her, warmly supporting and encouraging her, they also took time to coach Jeff and me on how we could best help Katie during this time.

As Katie's cries for help became more insistent, Ms. Amendola called me on my cell-phone, letting me know that it was important for us to meet together – Katie, me, Jeff, if he could make it, and Ms. Amendola. She understood the challenge of breaking away from Kevin and the hospital, and made time to meet whenever we could work her into our schedule.

Entering into the counseling area of Katie's school, I felt a warmth and compassion that was lacking in every other part of my world. Katie's counselor assured me that all of Katie's teachers had been made aware of her home situation. They were working with her on special test taking arrangements in case she had trouble concentrating. Katie could escape to the counseling center whenever she felt sad or afraid. Her experience was just the opposite of Phillip's, with her teachers working together to provide flexible assignment deadlines to account for our erratic schedules.

Katie had every type of support and encouragement possible from her school. But, Ms. Amendola let us know, we needed to offer her more support at home. Middle school was tough enough for girls, unstable home situations made their self-doubt and uncertainty more pronounced. Add in the type of disruption that had occurred for us and Katie was trying to deal with more emotional upheaval than she had the capacity to endure.

We were given a homework assignment. Buy a full-length mirror, Ms. Amendola told us. Write sticky notes to paste around the edges of the mirror so that each time Katie looked at the mirror, the notes would frame her face. Each sticky note should include something that we admired about Katie. We should include all of our family members in writing the notes of affirmation.

That afternoon Katie and I went to pick out a mirror. She didn't know the purpose of the mirror, but she was thrilled to have a chance to go shopping with me. Jeff hung the mirror that evening. When Katie woke up the next morning, she found two love notes attached to her mirror, one from me and one from Jeff. Slowly over the months that Kevin's illness continued, the mirror filled up with notes of the traits, memories, and abilities that make Katie special.

Ms. Amendola's lesson extended to Phillip as well. Jeff and I took turns leaving stickies at the head of Phillip's bed. He never mentioned receiving the notes, and we didn't flood his room with notes the way we did Katie's mirror. Yet, still today, the love notes exist on Phillip's bed and Katie's mirror as a reminder of how encouragement, compliments, and love became powerful allies for our family during Kevin's catastrophic illness.

My work situation was a different story entirely. I showed up for the meetings I was required to attend and did my best to focus on the content of the meetings. I learned that as long as I wasn't asked how *I* was doing, I could manage my emotions. When I was with Kevin, I stayed strong and encouraging so that he could draw his strength from me. During meetings at Phillip and Katie's schools, I kept my focus on the issues facing them, and controlled my emotions through that singular focus. At work I used this same strategy. Jeff and I spent our limited time together discussing plans of action, each of us locking our fears and sadness away so as not to put additional strain on each other.

And yet, on occasion, when I had a moment to myself, I would be overcome by the uncertainty, the fear, and the sadness of our situation. I would sit a few extra minutes alone in my car, the tears falling quietly, and some of the emotion built up behind my dam of strength would slip away. As I released some of my anxiety, I steeled myself to continue the fight.

One day during this time of despair, I broke down crying at work. I thought I was alone in a quiet hallway. I let down my emotional barrier, let the tears rain down my face, and sobbed out of exhaustion and confusion. Quietly, a long time colleague approached me and placed his hand on my shoulder. "I'm so sorry," he offered. I was confused. As the months progressed and the frustration of this silent, unnamed killer raged within Kevin, I had not heard from any of my close colleagues. Now it was clear that the awkward silences in the hallway, the odd absence of e-mails and calls weren't a result of lack of compassion.

The colleague was a person with whom I shared a deep and open friendship. He told me that he didn't know how to help me because he had heard rumors that Kevin was dying from anorexia. He felt at odds with what to say to me. And so I understood.

Had Kevin been fighting a different disease like cancer, my colleagues would have supported my family and me immediately, and in a multitude of ways. Later, once I knew how to communicate my needs, my colleagues supported me, but at first, we were a small island, my family and I, alone, day and night.

Kevin

I would wake up every day in extreme pain that wouldn't go away, with a tube shoved up my nose, and Ensure shoved down my stomach.

No one could tell me why.

No one could tell me what would make it change.

Everybody's parents probably have weird things that set them off. For my parents, it's when we say "can't" or "hate." When I was little and I'd be working on my homework, if I got mad and said, "I can't do this problem," my parents would freak.

"Maybe you 'won't,'" they would say, "but that doesn't mean you 'can't'."

Then they'd go all lecture-mode about how I could do anything I set my mind to. In their minds, as soon as the words "can't" left my mouth, I would be defeated.

I didn't understand what they meant then, but I do now. I guess it was a lot of the stuff that Coach Wooden had told me as well, when I saw him in California. All about giving everything no matter what, and everything. He said that giving 100 percent was what success meant.

The other word that was a swear word in our house was "hate." My brother would get my sister really mad by whispering, "I hate you," under his breath, and then she would go tell my parents, and they would come *unglued.*

My Mom would go on and on about how "hate" means you dislike somebody so much that you want to see that person *dead* and how my brother had *better* not be talking that way in *our* house.

So "hate" was definitely a bad word too.

When I came home from the hospital there were a lot of times that I really felt those words. They expressed so much of what I was feeling. And I just wanted to shout them out loud. But I didn't have the strength.

"Can't!"

"Hate!"

There were times that I knew that I was supposed to eat. On top of having a feeding tube, I was supposed to eat *more* food to make up for all the weight I had lost.

Most of the time after my mom would make me these special waffles with oil and peanut butter, I would take two bites and tell her, "I can't take another bite."

Or my dad would make me milkshakes with half and half and whole milk and Cold Stone Ice Cream and it would be like, "No, I can't."

And they never got mad at me for saying, "I can't." Not even if I told them, "I can't," when they got me up to go to school, or if I called them after I had gone to half of a class and said, "I can't make it through the rest of the day."

It seems like I lived in a *world* of can't when I got out of the hospital.

I hated a lot of things too. I hated about every smell that existed. I hated the stupid tests that the doctors ran on me. And even though I got a bunch of attention when I showed up at school with my feeding tube the first day, I started hating my feeding tube after the first two days.

Normally my parents would have stopped me from all of the "I-hate-this" talk, and been like, "Well, that feeding tube is keeping you alive, so you don't have to like it, but you should appreciate what it is doing for you."

Or they would have been, "Those smells are dinner cooking for our family, so figure out how you are going to deal with them."

But they didn't.

I guess these were the signs, again, of how bad off I was. Or maybe they tried to get me to stop saying "can't" and "hate" like they always did, and maybe I just don't remember.

All I know is that when I came home from the hospital, I hated a lot of things about my life. And I felt like there was no way that I could do the stuff that all of my friends were doing.

It was total "can't" and "hate," and it sucked.

Every morning I would wake up with that tube up my nose, and I would have to try to eat again. And they would tell me to take more pills, and everyone would try to figure out whether I could just make the pain go away if I quit thinking about it or if I quit worrying.

What if I just quit caring?

Or if I just quit living?

Then the pain would go away, right?

Mom

I was scared. I still didn't know what was wrong with Kevin, despite his unceasing pain. He seemed to have lost his will to live, and the doctors had quit trying to figure out what was wrong with him and could only recommend that he take more of the drugs that weren't working.

It was hard to do any kind of "normal" tasks, from meeting with my kids' teachers to facing the crowds at their concerts and events. I couldn't even bear the questions I would be asked at the grocery store. It was so difficult to tell the entire story *again*, and to relive the horror over and over.

On top of the emotional challenge of explaining Kevin's health status, there would come a point in each conversation when people wanted to know what was wrong with Kevin. How was I supposed to explain that we didn't know what was wrong? It seemed wrong to seek prolonged support and empathy from people when I didn't even know what to tell them was wrong, or how long we expected to be living under this dark cloud.

So it was a blessing in disguise when Kevin was discharged from the hospital with a feeding tube in his stomach. We knew that at the very least he was getting nutrition. It was outward proof of his inner battle, even serving to give Kevin "street credibility" at school, showing his friends that indeed there was really something wrong with him, even though it did not yet have a name.

I was simply trying my best to keep Kevin alive. This seemingly simple task took up most of my waking hours, especially when a feeding tube was added to the demands. Learning how to manage his feeding tube and adjust how many calories he could endure was tough. Just getting Kevin out of the hospital proved more stressful than I could imagine. The afternoon came when Kevin was to leave. Discharge orders listed the medicines we were to manage, the medical provider that would be delivering the feeding tube equipment and recommendations for follow-up with Kevin's GI specialist.

Bringing Kevin home seemed straightforward until the last day in the hospital. Kevin's pain became worse, and his weight dipped to below pre-hospital levels and his legs began twitching. He became despondent, so we called his doctors. In the end they decided to keep Kevin in the hospital one final night. We had to know if he was going to be able to cope without morphine – the withdrawal from which could have been causing some of Kevin's symptoms. Kevin would need to be able to sleep comfortably at home, and he would have to consume enough calories through the feeding tube and orally to allow him to gain back the weight that continued to drop.

It was possible, our doctor said, that Kevin was suffering from *hospital-itis*, a discomfort that occurs when a patient had spent too much time in the hospital. One more night would allow the doctors and nurses a chance to monitor Kevin to see if he was stable enough to go home. Jeff stayed with Kevin the final night in the hospital.

At 11:00 the home phone rang.

"Kevin needs to talk to you," Jeff said. He handed the phone to Kevin.

So quietly I could barely hear him, Kevin cried, "Mommy, you have to come back to the hospital. My legs won't stay still. They hurt so bad. Please come back to rub them out and make me feel better."

Jeff got back on the line, "I don't know what to do."

"See if the doctors can get him some Benadryl," I suggested.

"They've already given him two." The quiet crying in the background ripped into my heart.

"Then ask for an Ambien. He has to get some sleep." We agreed that, short of narcotic pain medicine, we had asked for medicines that had helped Kevin through tough nights before.

The phone didn't ring again. The medicines allowed Kevin to get to sleep. And I could get a full night's sleep before Kevin arrived home with a feeding tube and a fistful of different medicines to manage.

The basics of feeding tube management were straightforward. Home health nurses showed Jeff and me how to fill the sterile plastic bag with Ensure, how to tape the tubing to Kevin's nose to avoid major chafing and how to run the pump that would feed Kevin much needed calories. Kevin's pump was to run 12 hours a day, ideally throughout the night so that he would not have to bring his pump with him to school.

The medicine line up was clear. Give Kevin an anti-depressant in the morning and night, increasing levels each week until they became therapeutic. Give Kevin anti-anxiety medicines at night because they would make him sleepy. Give Kevin anti-acids in the morning to offset his stomach acids and help his stomach recover from its "fried" (thin and covered with small *Petechiae*, or sores) state. Give Kevin anti-spasm medicines every 12 hours, with additional quick dissolving doses under his tongue if his pain became unbearable. Give Kevin narcotic pain medicine if his pain became unbearable and the relief from the anti-spasm medicines wasn't enough to allow him to eat and drink. Give Kevin sleeping aids if he was unable to go to sleep with the feeding tube running all night.

The first night and day seemed to go well enough. Kevin went to school with his feeding tube. He seemed relieved to have the outward evidence that something was medically wrong with him. He even wanted to bring his pump along with him to keep food going into his system the full 12 hours.

By the second and third day he started feeling worse. Nausea became his constant companion. His spirits tanked. He consumed less and less food orally. He begged me to turn off the feeding tube, because he could not get to sleep while it was running. As I watched Kevin's response to his home-from-the-hospital routine, it seemed as though Kevin's body was refusing the high number of calories pumped into his system. If the feeding pump ran the full 12 hours, Kevin would throw up additional food that he forced himself to eat.

I called the home health agency and asked what I should do. Helpful as the nurses wanted to be, they didn't have a solution. Perhaps he was nervous going back to school, they thought. Or perhaps some of the medicines he was taking were having an interaction affect. They couldn't tell me where to start.

Talking with Kevin, we made the decision to slow the pump rate and spread out the hours that he was hooked up to the pump. We changed the pump schedule to six hours on, six hours off. Kevin wasn't getting as many calories as before, but he did quit throwing up. To allow him to sleep, he would take a sleeping pill, and once he was soundly asleep, I would sneak into his room and set up the pump for six hours. On good nights Kevin was still asleep when I came in to turn the pump off six hours later. At school he would repeat the six-hour feeding process – on the days he felt well enough to attend school.

While my nights were broken up into schedules normally reserved for parents of a newborn, the sleep deprivation was worth it if it allowed Kevin to gain weight and feel better. Unfortunately, it didn't.

Over the next couple of weeks I filled and refilled Kevin's many prescriptions. I got to know our pharmacists quite well. Each additional refill and the accompanying consultation increased the level of the pharmacists' concern about the cocktail of medicines Kevin was on. Their concern mirrored my sense that the medicines did not seem to be making Kevin any better.

Our pharmacists' alarms about the myriad of drugs that were daily going into Kevin's system coincided with Kevin's response to the medicines. Kevin became despondent. He had no appetite. He had trouble sleeping and hated the times that the feeding tube was turned on, knowing that soon he would feel nauseated.

Dave and Robyn, two pharmacists at our local grocery store, became some of my most central confidants on Kevin's healthcare management team. In addition to the pharmacists, friends who had dealt with long-term chronic health issues pointed me to the National Institute of Health and other reputable research sites where I could begin to learn more about Kevin's symptoms, his medicines, and his prescribed treatments.

I studied each of the medicines Kevin was taking. I needed to know the potential side effects, and, more importantly, what their role was in healing Kevin. An acquaintance who had his Ph.D. in neurological medicines spent hours teaching me about the brain and the stomach's emotional receptors – how they worked and how the SSRIs (anti-depressants and anti-anxiety medicines) interacted with these receptors.

It was confusing, but I began to understand how the physicians thought these medicines could cure Kevin's "cycle of pain." Unfortunately, the cure would only work if Kevin was anxious and/or depressed.

In fact, it became obvious that the anti-spasm medicine was the only medicine giving Kevin actual relief from his pain. The narcotics prescribed masked Kevin's pain so that he could function and eat smoothies and drink Gatorade. The combination of anti-depressants and anti-anxiety medicines were a confusing mix of potentially helpful outcomes and dangerous side effects.

I took on the roles of head-nurse, occupational therapist, physical therapist, physician, and psychiatrist in order to manage Kevin's feeding tube, weight, and medicine dosages. On top of these roles, I researched new alternatives every day, convinced there was a better path to achieving health for my child.

We set up appointments with a social worker who had been kind and understanding in the hospital. We adjusted the speed and amount by which the Ensure was pumped into Kevin's thin frame so that it didn't threaten to come back out. We increased the medicine – waiting for the therapeutic levels to be reached and Kevin's pain to subside.

But his pain increased.

And, as drug levels increased, Kevin became more despondent.

For the first few days after getting out of the hospital, Kevin went to school, sat on the sidelines of his team's soccer games, and helped to set up a scary ghost for Halloween night. He looked forward to going trick-or-treating with his friends, but it was clear as the night came close that he just didn't have the strength. Each day, his energy decreased. The sparkle in his eye faded, and the strength and resolve with which he had been fighting faded.

It became more difficult to get him out of bed in the morning.

His humor evaporated, and he became a shell of our kid.

Desperately, Kevin declared he could not go on like this any longer. Our family of four gathered around him, held him tight and told him to do it for *us* – we would find out what was going on and fix it.

He only needed to focus on the next hour, the next day. I'm crying even now as I think back to those long nights.

Clearly, the path we were on was leading us further from health and closer to death. Jeff and I had discussions about hiding the knives and never leaving Kevin alone.

I took to sleeping next to Kevin so that I could hear his feeble heartbeat and calm him when he woke and cried out in the night. In those late night hours I would fire up my laptop and search the healthcare databases, studying harder than I ever had in my life, searching for a clue that I might have missed.

Kevin

So I just gave up.

It's crazy how my family knew.

They sat up with me all night. They told me all of the things that I had to live for.

They told me that if I didn't think I could live for *me*, maybe I could live for *them*.

Mom

I was desperate. And in my desperation, I turned once again to the search engines, hoping for a lead that would bring Kevin back from the brink of death and take away pain so great it made him contemplate taking his own life.

At our local pharmacy, the pharmacists helped me to understand the dangerous suicidal risks of anti-depressants for an individual who doesn't need them. Our pharmacists became so concerned that they contacted, on my behalf, another patient's mom who had also dealt with long-term abdominal pain issues with her son.

The more that I studied the potential causes of pain in the abdomen through different sources on the web and through the contacts we were referred to, the more convinced I became that something had been missed in Kevin's case. Clearly I wasn't in a position to determine what tests to run or how to solve Kevin's problem, but I began to realize that there were other options out there. These options gave me the speck of hope that we all needed.

I received an e-mail from Robyn, the mother about whom the pharmacists had spoken. They had contacted her, hoping that she could offer us ideas and support. She told me her son's story, how after years of watching him suffer from abdominal pain and the accompanying weight loss and emotional distress, she brought him to the University of Cincinnati Children's Hospital. The Cincinnati Hospital offered cutting edge interventions – Botox for abdominal pain, new medicines, and better diagnostic techniques.

It dawned on me that different hospitals and different doctors approached medical issues in different ways. As I explored gastric issues at the University of Cincinnati's Children's Hospital site, I learned that we could travel to Cincinnati to have Kevin seen by doctors who use cutting edge techniques to cure children of severe abdominal pain. I didn't know how we would pay for the expensive medical treatments they might offer, but I refused to let money stop me from healing my son.

As I listened to fellow moms, pharmacists, and the neurological researcher, I came to the realization that more of the same was certainly not the solution. These thin threads of hope breathed new life into Kevin's fight for a cure.

I began to see choices, and doors started very slowly to open for us.

In the months before Kevin's illness our family had planned a dream trip to New Zealand and Australia. Our trip was paid for, tickets and itinerary held in our safe. With all the stress, we had not thought to cancel the trip.

A week before our scheduled departure, Jeff reminded me that we could cancel the trip up until 24 hours prior with an emergency medical reason. It was evident to all of us that Kevin was in no condition to travel, but in our preoccupation with all that was going on, we had still never gotten around to cancelling the vacation.

I had recently located a new medicine that would treat "abdominal migraines" that was currently available in Australia but not in the United States, since the FDA had not yet approved it. The medicine also had the side effect of weight-gain, something we would welcome in Kevin, to say the least.

We now saw those tickets for our family trip as a potential new beginning for Kevin. We could visit a major center for neural gastroenterological study, which just happened to be located in Australia, where doctors were versed in explanations for Kevin's pain.

Our trip would serve many purposes. First, doctors not biased by Kevin's medical record would see Kevin, and specialists not constrained by America's healthcare system could offer their ideas. The trip would also provide us access to the new medicine that, at the very worst, might increase his weight.

The only hurdle left to face was to convince Kevin that he needed to summon the strength for a trip halfway around the world.

Kevin

A long time ago my Mom had planned to go to Australia, but we all figured it was cancelled since I was so sick.

Then I gave up living.

Mom was always online looking for some kind of cure for me, and she found some new medicines and some different doctors in Australia, and then she started trying to convince me.

One night she got me online with her and showed me the information about the medicine and started talking about how sometimes kids have abdominal migraines, and since our family had lots of migraines maybe mine just came in my gut.

I wasn't in very good shape, and it was hard for me to think about it, and I definitely didn't know if I wanted to get in an airplane. But I thought there wasn't much to lose anyway. And besides that, mom started making sense.

I decided that maybe there was something over across the ocean worth me staying alive.

We decided that we would go to New Zealand and Australia.

CHAPTER FIVE

Down Under to Come Up

(December 2007)

Kevin

It was jellyfish season on the Great Barrier Reef, so we wore these bright blue lycra suits that looked like kiddie pajamas with footies, mittens and a hood.

The sun beat down on Mom and me, and we kicked our fins through dozens of brightly colored fish while the current pulled us way away from the Quicksilver catamaran.

Under the water it was so quiet. I had been afraid that I wouldn't be strong enough to handle the ocean, but I was out there with the coral reef and the sharks and the turtles.

Mom

Just getting on the airplane in Los Angeles with the post 9/11 travel restrictions created entirely new and unexpected challenges. Kevin required a wheelchair to move between gates and terminals, there were long lines to clear security, and it was necessary to carry signed doctor's orders in order to carry special liquids on board the plane.

Kevin's medicines required refrigeration for the 15-hour flight, and Kevin would need a place to lie prone should an episode of pain occur during the flight.

Despite the many difficulties, upon every step of the journey kind, helpful employees from a variety of agencies and companies met us. The airport security officers pulled us out of the security line and escorted us through the scanner. Quantas Airlines located a row with the only remaining empty seat so that Kevin could lie flat in my lap for the duration of the flight, and flight attendants cleared a cooler for his medicine.

We reaped great rewards visiting New Zealand and Australia. We looked at Kevin's health from a new perspective and observed his symptoms objectively. After a period of intense darkness and stress, we connected as a family in settings of beauty and charm.

Kevin

We went to the Great Barrier Reef for two days. And they were the best days of my life. Mostly. Last year my English teacher had us write an essay on our best day ever. I wrote an essay on spending a day at the Great Barrier Reef.

But it was hard to pick just one day out of an incredible three and a half week trip and say that was the best day. Especially when I went from literally wanting to die to doing the most amazing things in the world overnight. How could I ever just pick one day?

Mom

It would have been impossible for Kevin to survive the flight halfway across the world without the support of his local medical team. I contacted the GI specialist who was overseeing Kevin's case at the time to check with him on the medicine and specialists

I had located in Australia and New Zealand.

The doctor was intrigued and even supportive of our taking the trip. He ran through the limited options that he felt remained for Kevin in the States. We could try new mood-altering medicines, perhaps, and continue to strengthen Kevin via a feeding tube. With no other clear plan of action, the specialist gave us his blessing for our journey. He filled out the special forms we needed for the flight and provided a letter of introduction to doctors we might see during the trip.

We would need to carry Kevin's liquid diet with us, which required special clearance for airport security processes. We needed access to wheelchairs and even special medications should the long flight become unbearable for Kevin.

Just a few days later, we found ourselves as a family, sitting nervously on an airplane. Jeff and I anxiously assured ourselves that we could hop on a flight right back home should we find that we had made the wrong decision. Instead, it became apparent the very first day that we had made the right decision.

The morning we arrived in New Zealand, Jeff took off to see the sights of Christchurch with Phillip and Katie. Kevin and I followed them into town later, allowing Kevin a chance to rest. When we met up with Phillip and Katie in the downtown square in the afternoon, Kevin realized that he was missing out on some serious fun at the science museum, so he looked past his pain and we stepped up the pace a bit.

The first hope of this trip had already been realized. Kevin had a focus outside of that pain in his gut. He began to live again. Each day, Kevin continued to fight through the pain and move away from the depths of his emotional despair.

With new exciting activities to occupy his mind each day, Kevin's pain was no longer the center of his life. He certainly was not suddenly a strong, strapping young lad. He was still very ill, but we declared victory for the little battle we had won. We were now once again able to think about living.

Kevin

I was out there on the Great Barrier Reef, and I wasn't thinking about anything except the fish and the coral and the sun. It was so amazing.

Time flew by.

I would point out a huge fish or turtle to Mom and she would point out a cool shark or eel to me.

Before I knew it Mom tapped me on my arm. We had kicked ourselves so far away from the main boat that the crew had sent a Zodiac with *surfsavers* (that's what they call their lifeguards in Australia) to bring us back.

The whole trip was like that – incredible.

At home I had spent days and days in the hospital, and when I wasn't in the hospital, I had still had tubes and needles shoved into me most days for the past 10 weeks. And I kept getting worse.

And no one could tell me what was wrong with me except that I was stuck in some cycle of pain and that I needed to figure out how to make myself eat. And I needed to be less stressed out about soccer and school.

Even though we still went to the doctors and I still got sick during the trip, I felt like I had left my troubles behind me.

Mom

In addition to having lively activities to engage Kevin – things that he didn't want to miss out on – we were also able see the pattern of Kevin's ailment. We came to understand the intermittent nature of Kevin's pain, the intensity of the episodes.

Back home, caught in the confines of daily routines, perhaps Kevin had become worried about the next episode and so depressed by the medications that his symptoms were confusing. We had become bewildered as to what were Kevin's symptoms and what was the cause of his pain. Breaking away from the hospitals, the ever-changing medicines and procedures, and the constant doctors visits at least allowed us to get a sense of the patterns of Kevin's pain.

We also were able to see what foods Kevin could tolerate, how much he could eat and what occurred after he ate. Without the feeding tube and without access to a regular kitchen, Kevin could tune in to what his body told him he needed. He was back to pancakes, Rice Krispies cereal and peanut butter and jelly sandwiches rather than a feeding tube pumping Ensure into his body.

And each night I plotted a connection with the foreign healthcare system so that we could obtain a prescription for the medicine I wanted Kevin to try as soon as possible.

The first four days of our trip, we journeyed to spectacular hot springs, travelled across mountains and through valleys between Christchurch and Grey's Harbor on one of the "Five Most Beautiful Train Rides" in the world (according to *National Geographic*), and cruised down the western shoreline of the South Island of New Zealand. We stopped to snap hundreds of photos, as each bend along the road opened up to more and more spectacular scenery.

Our trip itinerary called for us to spend a few days exploring the glacier region of the South Island. Since we had a home base for a few days, this afforded an opportunity to see a specialist. We had tried at Grey's Harbor, but the short time span of our visit and their lack of specialists meant that the local clinic couldn't help us in the small ocean front town. Further south we had time to work through the New Zealand healthcare system.

As we pulled into the parking lot of the health clinic in the small town of Franz Josef late one evening my hopes of finding any healthcare providers still around were dim. I had heard rumors that it took a long time to get an appointment with a doctor in foreign countries where healthcare was provided for every citizen. To my surprise, a woman stepped out of the closed healthcare facility and asked if she could help me. She introduced herself as the area nurse.

I explained our situation. She told me that the specialists we needed to see would be found in Queenstown, a four-hour drive south (and the next town we were planning to visit). She warned me that I should call ahead to make an appointment, for just as I had suspected, getting an appointment could be difficult.

"Sometimes it can take two days to get in to see a physician if you aren't in desperate straights," she warned me. "If you call today it might be late tomorrow afternoon before you can see anyone." A whole day's wait was the nurse's interpretation of "a long time to get an appointment with a specialist." Goodness, what a relief.

The doctor assessed Kevin physically, listened to his story carefully, then sought to understand the situation from my perspective while Kevin fell asleep on the examining table in the background. After asking pointed questions and briefly reviewing Kevin's record, she told me that she was not in a position to make a decision about dispensing the medicine on her own; she needed to meet with her team of doctors.

She was honest and upfront about her concerns about dispensing the medication. She said she would not be available to follow up with the medicine and if it did work, how would Kevin continue to get a supply of the medicine to stay healthy? Finally, she wasn't convinced there was enough evidence that the medicine would treat his health problem.

Her forthright way of dealing with her concerns was so refreshing that I left the appointment not frustrated or anxious, but assured that the matter was being given the best consideration possible.

We were to come back in two days at which time she would have assembled a team of six doctors to review Kevin's case and have arrived at a decision. She kept Kevin's entire medical file with a promise that she would keep everything together and return it at our follow-up appointment. I trusted her.

When we first checked in for our appointment, the front desk staff person was very apologetic when she informed us we would have to pay for our visit. I let them know that I expected this, and they told me to expect a $40 charge. Upon leaving, we were told that because the doctor had not actually been able to help us at that appointment there was no charge. No charge! What a difference in comparison to the American healthcare system.

In two days time, true to her word, our New Zealand doctor showed us the notes from the review board and informed us that she still was not convinced that the medicine would treat Kevin's problem. After reviewing his file she thought perhaps some diagnostics had not been conducted that would help to understand what was going on inside Kevin's abdomen.

Still, if we would get Kevin off of all anti-depressants and anti-anxiety medicines (and she told us how to do this over the next couple of months), then we could start him on a low dose of Pizotifen, a medicine prescribed for abdominal migraines, available in Australia and New Zealand, but not in the United States. Hopefully this medicine would have a side effect of weight gain, and might possibly, if his problem was indeed abdominal migraines, help him to feel better. She could write a prescription for three months and we could get an additional prescription in Australia for more months. That would buy us time to figure out what was going on with Kevin.

This New Zealand Healthcare appointment cost us next to nothing and was, in fact, the roadmap that we followed to bring Kevin back to health. I can't imagine a wiser $40 I've ever spent.

Kevin

Phillip, Katie, and I were playing in the waves at Noosa Head Beach when I had this one really bad episode. That was really scary.

My dad had to go back home to the United States early to get back to his business, so it was just Mom and us kids.

We were staying close to the beach, and Mom checked with us like a hundred thousand times to see if it would be okay if she got a massage the afternoon before we were supposed to fly home. There were lifeguards there, we were all teenagers, and we thought it was kind of silly how worried she was about leaving us at this beach for an hour while she walked to get a massage.

She probably felt horrible when she came back to find me stretched out at the surfsaver station with an oxygen mask strapped to my face.

Phil was running to our apartment to grab my medicine and Katie was sitting next to me trying to make me feel better. Mom had barely left my side for the past three months, and after this episode, she didn't leave my side for the next year and a half.

Mom

We didn't get the answer we had hoped to find. The medicine was not the magic cure I had hoped it might be. Kevin did not mysteriously stop getting his episodes of pain and suddenly begin eating like the teenagers that surrounded him in his daily life.

However, the trip did provide many insights into what was going on with Kevin. And it allowed us to move out of the dark place where we had been residing and shine a bright optimistic light on life.

We laughed and enjoyed our time together as a family and remembered that there was much to live for. We firmly believed that the pain would eventually go away, and Kevin would get well.

The doctors we visited in both New Zealand and Australia provided new ideas for paths to follow upon our return. These paths included diagnostics that might have been left undone due to our over-burdened "horses not zebras" healthcare system. Also, alternative modalities, including acupuncture and massage allowed Kevin to deal with his pain in alternative ways until we were able to determine the cause of his pain.

The trip was far from easy. And yet, of all of the journeys we've taken as a family, this trip provides the warmest glow inside my heart.

From the darkest place in my life, this trip brought me back out into the light.

Kevin

Mostly a lot of good things came out of the trip down-under. Like me wanting to go on living.

I got to go to the animal preserve and play with kangaroos and hold koala bears. I still wasn't very strong, so after I had played with the kangaroos and fed them, I lay down next to a kangaroo and fell right to sleep with my arms wrapped around his neck.

But the best day of my life was at the Great Barrier Reef. It was more than just the awesome fish and coral that we saw when we were there.

I think it was really about leaving the hospital and feeding tubes behind.

CHAPTER SIX

A Dose of Reason

(December 2007 – March 2008)

Mom

Our trip *Down Under* did a lot of good things for our family. We spent time having fun together. We had a new plan to cure Kevin. We got a break from day-in and day-out medical care. But the stress over Kevin's diminished health continued to keep everyone in the family on high alert. It was a long journey from the sunny beaches of Australia to the snowbound roadside where I threw Phillip out of the car into a snow bank in the middle of a raging snowstorm. At that point, I probably should have realized I needed some help to cope with the crisis in our lives.

Poor Phil. I cannot justify the way I treated him that cold, blizzardy day. Without thinking, I unleashed my fury on my stoic 16-year-old son. Maybe I read his self-assured teenaged *know-it-all-facade* as a safe place to release my frustration.

Phil was old enough to drive himself to school, but not in the middle of a blizzard. A foot and a half of new snow had already accumulated on the highway with not a snowplow in sight. I had to drive Phil to high school.

The frequency of Kevin's episodes and the status of his low weight kept me on guard all the time. I allowed myself one release during these demanding days, my Friday morning dance class, my only indulgence. On this particular morning I needed to get Phil to school before I would be free to dance. Afterward, I would return to Kevin and all my worries.

And the snow got in our way.

We crept along, four miles per hour, bumper to bumper with dozens of other cars inching their way into town.

The stress inside me grew as the clock on the dashboard ticked toward the starting time of my dance class. An irrational fire burned in me.

I had missed the warm up. Tears formed.

Another minute spent trapped by cars and snow; dancing started without me. I pulled off to the side of the road and yelled at Phil, "Get out."

His big eyes looked back at me, not the eyes of a 16-year-old, but the worried eyes of my older son: questioning, imploring, and doing as he was told.

He pulled his hood up over his head, gathered his backpack from the back hatch of the car and turned to walk the final mile toward school.

Three steps into his walk I dashed out of the car, ran to him, and hugged him. I handed him the keys and told him to drive. I wasn't able to at that moment.

As Phil settled into the driver's seat to drive us through the snow, my cell phone rang. It was Jeff.

Phil answered the phone.

"No," Phil said. "She can't talk right now. She's busy."

He didn't mention that I was busy sobbing.

It began to dawn on me that my need to be independently strong was hurting me and hurting our family. And so began the next phase of my learning.

I learned how to be vulnerable. Of the myriad of lessons I learned throughout Kevin's healthcare crisis, perhaps this lesson took the longest for me to learn.

Kevin

I didn't want to come back.

I wanted to stay in Australia, live with the kangaroos and hang out on a quiet beach.

I liked that the doctors had listened to me, even though they couldn't tell me what was wrong with me.

I liked having all day to sip on some Gatorade and take a few bites of pancakes or French fries. I liked not having smells fill up my nose making me feel worse.

The times *Burnie* (the pain in my stomach) got really mad weren't as bad when we were in Australia. At home I would lie downstairs on the couch with nothing to do but think about my pain.

On our trip I could take my Hyoscyamine, the one medicine that helped me feel a little bit better, wait for it to start working and for the worst part of the pain to pass. Afterward I could rest or go somewhere fun and beautiful to take my mind off of my body. Best of all, I always had my family around me.

Every day in Australia and New Zealand, the only people who understood how much I was hurting were right there with me. They would stop the car and wait for me to feel better. Or I could stay behind at the hotel with Mom and catch up with Dad, Phil and Kate when I felt better.

And the doctors told me what I could do to start feeling better.

They told me to stop taking the anti-depressants and the anti-anxiety medicines. They told me how to slowly cut back on how much I was taking. They said it would take a long time to get all of the medicine out of my body before I could try the new medicine that we got. But it was a plan. I liked that there was a plan.

But we had to come home sometime.

At home were all the smells that made me feel like I was going to throw up.

Dad is a really good cook. He likes to cook with onions.

For me, onions were the worst. When Dad would make onion soup for the family, I would hide downstairs.

I would get as far from the kitchen as I could, scratch an orange and put the peel up to my nose so I wouldn't throw up.

Mom

The glow from the Southern Hemisphere remained on my skin, yet it dissipated from my soul shortly after our return to the cold, short days of our mountain home. The holidays were upon us. Usually we spent the time with my extended family gathered in my parents' home. The holiday would be different this year.

We stayed in a friend's home near my folks because Kevin needed rest. My parents' crowded house would be too much for Kevin to handle. For him to participate in the days' events would be enough.

Our friends told us that a special heating system would keep the house at a comfortable temperature. We were asked not to touch the thermostats. Fair enough.

Kevin and I tucked ourselves into bed, our dog at our feet.

The night got longer. Our bodies grew colder. The dog climbed under the covers.

I searched the closets and robbed blankets from other beds.

Morning came and I checked the temperature. The thermometer in the house hovered near 50.

At that point, Kevin was so painfully thin that the only place he had been truly warm was in Australia's 100-degree heat. In the night he had shivered mercilessly under the covers.

I had to do something. I couldn't force Kevin to live through another night of cold. But what could I do? I already felt like a complainer who didn't want to stay with everyone else.

The next day I told my brother how the cold house had kept us awake half the night.

No sooner than I mentioned the problem to him, it was solved. My brother and parents headed out to the house where the temperature now had dropped into the 40's.

Even on Christmas Day, Dad, the ultimate problem solver, was able to get a friend of his in town to take a look at the system to determine the problem (no fuel).

Fuel would not be delivered on Christmas, but portable heaters could be set up.

My family helped me when I needed it. Of course they did. So why did I have such a hard time asking for what I needed?

Why was it so hard to keep people informed about what was going on? I had to figure out a way to communicate what we needed from other people. I had to learn to ask for help.

It was the only way we could survive this crisis.

Kevin

I wished I were back in Australia where it was warm.

It was cold when we got home. I couldn't get warm. I would

turn on our gas fireplaces, and Mom would turn up the thermostat in the house to 74 degrees. Everyone else would come home and put on shorts while I would cover up with a big comforter on our downstairs couch.

That's pretty much the way I spent most of my days. When I got up, Mom would make me a protein smoothie, or she would try to get me to drink an Odwalla protein drink. I guess the Odwalla drinks are full of calories. I really got sick of how they tasted after a few weeks though, and told Mom and Dad to quit buying them for me.

The table next to me was covered with animal crackers and short bread cookies. There was red Gatorade and protein drinks. I would just try to take as many bites and sips as I could. Mom would sit across from me working on her laptop. We'd have *The Office* or *Scrubs* playing on the TV and every few hours I would take a pain pill or a pill that was supposed to stop spasms in my stomach to keep *Burnie* from making me crazy.

The fewer of the anti-depressants I took, the more I started to feel better. My pain didn't go away, but I started to get myself out of bed in the morning. I would take showers if my parents reminded me that I should. I could walk further with my dad when he would come home from work, and I started to go to school more. I even felt like going to my grandparents' for Christmas.

Christmas at my grandparents didn't turn out to be the happiest Christmas I ever had. Usually getting together with all of my cousins is fun. We sled and go to movies and play games like Sardines where one person hides and when you find that person you hide with them until everyone is crammed into the hiding spot together. This year I didn't feel good enough to play the games. I didn't even want to be in the same house where all of my cousins had their sleepovers with Grammie and Papa. It was too hard to see how much fun they were all having while I just hurt.

I couldn't even make it through a movie. Us older cousins went to see Will Smith's movie, *I Am Legend.* I wanted to see the movie ever since my brother Phil told me how cool it was. The movie was cool, but halfway through I couldn't stand it; I called Mom and told her to please come pick me up. She did, right away, and we went back out to the quiet house that some friends of my grandparents let us use so I could get away from all of the smells and sounds. I don't know why I wanted to be out at the quiet house, but I just felt better out there where I could sleep a lot or read and snuggle with my dog, Cooie.

When Mom and I were staying out at the quiet house we decided that I should take a couple of months off of going to the doctors and having tests done. Instead we decided that I would work to get off all of the medicines that I was on. Once I was off all of the other medicines, I would try the Pizotofen that we got on our trip and see if things would get better. I liked this plan.

I had to go back to school.

School was so hard. I was too tired to make it through the day. The lunchroom smelled terrible. All of the kids running around the halls would make me sad because I didn't feel good enough to even walk, and they all could run and laugh.

I would go to only two classes, English and science. The teachers in these classes were the best.

My English teacher, Mrs. Clarke, would come to my house to make sure I was still learning English. She would show up with her twins and a box of surprises. She made CDs of the books we were reading in class so that I could listen to them. And she had cards that my friends in the class had made.

The first time she came over to bring me stuff to work on so that I could pass 8th grade, she had tears in her eyes when she came into my room. It was weird to think that a teacher would cry when she saw me, but Mrs. Clark was a really special teacher who cared a ton.

Mrs. Proffit was my science teacher. Since we had a lot of labs and stuff that we could only do in class, she would make sure that my friends took good notes and helped me figure out what we were learning. Science is my favorite class, and all of my friends were in there with me, so I hated to miss class. I tried as hard as I could to finish that class so that I could go to high school the next year. I couldn't even imagine missing that.

I also had a tutor, Sue, who would come to my house to teach me math and geography. Sue used to be a teacher. She is like an Aunt to me. She seemed to know what days I felt good enough to think and what days I needed my Mom sitting next to me to make it through the lesson.

During the Christmas break I would go up to my neighbor's house and she would teach my friend Tanner and me. My neighbor was really sick with Crohn's Disease and would sometimes get pneumonia because his body was so weak.

Tanner and I had been friends since second grade, but he had been sick for so long I hadn't seen him much. So on the days when I felt good enough to go to Tanner's, or he was well enough to have me come up to learn with him, it was good to hang out with someone else.

I feel really bad for saying this, but I felt jealous of Tanner sometimes. He knew what was wrong with him. His disease was scary and bad, but at least he knew what was making him feel so bad.

I would go up to his house and try to learn geography, but then his mom would make up a big batch of chocolate fudge and the smell would make me feel awful. I would call my Mom to come get me. And I still didn't know why I felt so awful.

Mom

After the holidays I started teaching an overload schedule at the college, per my contract. I continued fulfilling the executive coaching contracts I had signed prior to Kevin's illness.

I discussed with human resource personnel the necessity of carefully evaluating when and if I should take advantage of the Family Medical Leave Plan. This legislative sponsored plan, which is guaranteed to employees should they encounter a family medical emergency, allows employees to take an unpaid leave from their position, retain their health benefits for up to three months, and return to their same position.

I would only be allowed to use the plan one time each year. When using the plan, not only would I forego my salary, I would also be responsible for complete coverage of my health insurance premiums ($1500/month). It was impossible to know when and if Kevin's health was going to get better or diminish, so if I used the plan now and his health declined later, then I would be left in a more desperate situation.

Any action that could put our health insurance and income at risk was unacceptable to me. This included doing anything less than what I had committed to in the classroom along with continued research and publication. And so I soldiered on with my prior commitments.

Besides losing weight, I was also losing my sense of humor, my ability to think rationally, and quite likely, my mind.

Each day I managed to function by focusing only on the most urgent task in front of me. I kept my focus strictly on outward issues that needed my attention, and, for the most part, I was so buried by commitments that I had little time to vent my emotions.

At night I couldn't sleep. My brain would needle at Kevin's problems all night long. At home I helped my children with homework, drove car pools, and thought of nothing beyond what was necessary to get through the next day.

An emotional distance grew between Jeff and me. I threw the weight of my uncertainty and doubt at Jeff.

When Jeff listened to the doctors and weighed the merits of their conclusion that Kevin might be suffering from anxiety, I railed against him as a traitor.

When Jeff had tried to take over the night management of Kevin's feeding pump, I oversaw his efforts and belittled each of the same mistakes I had made in my early attempts.

When Jeff worried about the dangers of Kevin becoming addicted to the narcotic pain medicine the doctors prescribed, I acted as an expert on the subject, repeating what the doctors had told me about the need to control the pain, and the low risks of addiction at the levels Kevin was consuming. I did not listen to Jeff's deeper concerns about being left out of the decision making process of Kevin's health.

We went from being a team in Kevin's recovery to people living on two opposing islands.

We had been each other's best friend, discussing our areas of difference, coming to an agreement about raising our children, spending our money and balancing our careers. Now in my mind, Jeff became part of the problem.

I rationalized that he didn't spend as much time with Kevin, so he couldn't possibly understand what medicine Kevin needed. He wasn't able to make it to all of the appointments, so I lorded around like the medical expert. Kevin wanted me next to him, so I prided myself on the singularly important role I played in Kevin's life.

But, of course, Jeff was affected by Kevin's illness as deeply as

I was. Each day he went to work, asking his employees if they had any leads on good doctors, checking with his physician clients for ideas they might have to cure Kevin. And he kept the house running and in order, dealing with medical bills and hot water heater breakdowns, lawn mowing and car repairs.

I felt overwhelmed. I was up to my eyeballs in medical care, overtime work commitments and managing Phillip and Katie's educations. With all that we had needing attention, I thought Jeff had lost his mind when he announced that we should pick out new carpet for our upstairs family room and have our hardwood floors refinished.

I could live with the gaping hole where we had worn the carpet down to the carpet pad. The warped areas and scratches on our hardwood floor were irrelevant to me. I looked past the carpet and hardwood floors to what seemed the 'right' priorities for our family.

Each time Jeff brought up looking at carpet or calling a hardwood company, I tossed obstacles in his way. How on earth could Jeff seriously think about choosing carpet, disrupting our home with workers, filling our home with smells that Kevin could not tolerate, and leaving me to care for Kevin in our basement as workers crawled over our upstairs? And how could he justify the expense of hardwood repair and carpet when we were up to our necks in medical bills? But Jeff wouldn't let go of the carpet.

To say this brought about a fight between us would be wrong. Neither Jeff nor I are fighters in the traditional sense. We don't raise our voices, we don't throw things, and we don't yell or get angry. Perhaps we should, but we don't.

Instead we engaged in a fight of silence. Clipped conversations replaced discussions about important topics. We avoided topics that would cause strain – the kids, the house, and worst of all, Kevin's ongoing suffering.

Looking back, I am embarrassed by my unyielding sense of

control. At the time I was so engrossed in Kevin's illness that I could not see how keeping such a tight grip on my emotions was eating me alive from the inside.

It was the distancing from Jeff that finally brought me to my knees. I needed him by my side if we were to get Kevin well. Only I couldn't see that at the time.

Spring was coming to the mountains. Spring, the time of rebirth, newness, sunshine, and opportunity. Surely spring would fill the emotional void that turned each day into a balancing act for me. I buried my emotions deep inside to create stability for my children, careful to not explode. I feared the emotions would tip me off to one side, and I would fall deep into the abyss of despair that existed on either side.

But spring made things worse. Kevin tried to play soccer, but did little more than sit on the sidelines, buried in his heavy winter coat. Katie took up lacrosse which added the obligation of carpooling to my long list of to do's. Phillip invited groups of his high school friends over to the house, adding a constant cacophony of hungry, messy teens to the mix.

Meanwhile Jeff and I stepped gingerly around each other.

Grabbing more junk food at the store to keep on hand for the teens, I crossed paths with a psychiatrist I had worked with following a mild stroke I had suffered a few years earlier.

Robyn and I had become friends, coming out of our counseling sessions, but our paths rarely crossed. As she greeted me, the compassion in her eyes touched my heart. My eyes welled with tears.

"What's going on, Vicki? It's been so long since I've seen you around town." Her concern for me caused my tears to overflow.

"Oh, Robyn, Kevin is so sick and I don't know what to do." It was all I could say.

"Call me."

I called. Maybe Robyn could talk to Kevin, I thought. She knew our family. Perhaps she could get inside his head to determine whether he was plagued by uncertainty and doubt. At the very least I thought she might be able to provide strength and a safe harbor for Kevin to turn to when the pain became too much.

But she made it clear that she wasn't the right person to help Kevin, though she could help *me.*

Robyn talked with me about taking an anti-depressant that had helped me recover from the mild stroke that had originally brought me to her as a patient. The medicine helped me move out of the dark tunnel of hopelessness I felt trapped in. Best of all, with it I got some much-needed sleep.

The most lasting tool Robyn provided, though, was an ability to understand the differences that were causing friction between Jeff and me. When I met with Robyn, I railed on about Jeff's desire to replace the carpet and fix the hardwood.

I asked her what could be wrong with a person so out of touch with what was happening around the house that he would conduct disruptive house repairs in the middle of his son's catastrophic illness? It sounds silly, but I really couldn't let go of the idea that Jeff was completely out of touch with Kevin's illness. How could he care more about the house than his son? Quite frankly, I was angry. He was missing the whole urgency of Kevin's health crisis if all he could focus on was carpet.

"Look at it this way," Robyn explained. "You are setting up the appointments with the doctor, following up on the procedures, taking action."

Thank heavens, she gets how tough I have it, I thought. *She knows how hard I'm working to get Kevin well. She's on my side and realizes that Jeff is completely off base.*

"Jeff is feeling helpless." Robyn continued.

Oh, dear, I thought. Now I'm going to have to take care of one more person's needs. Go ahead; stick Jeff's helplessness on me. I'm strong, I can handle it.

"He needs to have some control over something," she said. Her voice of reason did not yet reach me.

She went on, "He is as affected by all of this as you are. If you won't let him handle Kevin's health, then he will take control of the house."

Finally, the light bulb flashed on in my mind. Jeff was Kevin's parent, too. Robyn helped me put in place a plan where I could unload some of the responsibilities I was hoarding onto Jeff. Jeff needed to be part of Kevin's team, and I needed Jeff to support us.

"When was the last time you cried with Jeff?"

Whew, Robyn hit a nerve here. I didn't cry about Kevin with Jeff at all. In fact, I did my best not to cry in front of anyone – especially our family. By being strong I felt I was lending my strength to those around me.

Robyn helped me see that bottling up all of my emotion was creating additional stress on those around me. I was becoming unpredictable and irrational. I needed to let go, not of the fight for Kevin's life, but of my belief that I was the only person that could find a cure.

Slowly I eased into a new way of looking at how to get Kevin well. Instead of replacing the carpet, Jeff and I started working as a team to figure out Kevin's problem.

Jeff runs a medical billing company and has access to many of the best doctors, procedures, and insurance policies. He knows the language and the people. And Jeff was ahead of me in his openness to alternative modalities. For example, he worked with Kevin to see an acupuncturist.

If the insurance company denied a treatment, Jeff followed up to understand why. When we needed a recommended specialist, Jeff knew how to get us in for an appointment. Jeff could be rational with the doctors who had pushed me so far over the emotional line that I couldn't deal with them. I was too defensive. Together, we started to make progress in the fight for an answer to Kevin's illness.

Along with my change in attitude, I leveled with my colleagues at work. Administrators who did not even know my son was ill came to my rescue. They relieved me of administrative duties and made adjustments to my summer teaching load.

We figured out that I could drop to a three-fourths contract for the upcoming school year rather than deal with the uncertainty of utilizing the Family Medical Leave Act. This solution left my health insurance intact, while lightening my workload.

As I started to share the truth of our situation, colleagues who had dealt with health issues as severe as Kevin's passed along their coping techniques. I learned about resources including *CaringBridge.org* so that I could keep individuals updated on our status without having to tell the story over and over. *CaringBridge.org* became a link to enlist support crews to provide family meals and encouragement.

Katie continued to work with the counselors in her school, unloading the "emotional rocks" she packed in her backpack when it got too heavy for her to carry around. Her counselor, Ms. Amendola, provided her with love and support every day.

And Phil? Well, Phil and I began to chuckle about the way I had unfairly abused him that snowy day on the way to school. One time I jokingly asked why he made me miss my dance class. He said, "Mom, you're such a bad dancer, the class wouldn't have helped you anyway."

Kevin

When I finally stopped taking the anti-depressants and the anti-anxiety medicines, I would sometimes feel like meeting my friends at the ski area. I could only make it down one or two easy green slopes, but my friends loved having me around at lunchtime. My parents would always give me plenty of money to buy lunch, and they told me to order whatever I thought I could eat. I would order a big plate of mashed potatoes and some French fries. After a few bites, I couldn't eat any more, so my friends would fight over who got to eat the rest of the food I had left.

Slowly I started to take the Pizotifen instead of the anti-depressants. I was pretty excited since I hoped these would show us that I was just having bad stomach migraines. Once the new medicine from Australia started working, I could see myself trying out for the soccer team and going to soccer camps in the summer. I couldn't wait to start feeling normal again.

But the new medicine didn't make *Burnie* go away.

And now my Mom went into overdrive. Instead of going back to our GI specialist that helped us earlier, she lined up meetings with so many doctors I don't think I can remember them all. The first doctor's appointment after my little break from the medical system was horrible. I had to go back to the hospital. The smells were the worst.

I stepped into the entryway and it hit me – that awful hospital smell.

I told Mom and Dad that I couldn't go through with it. We had to leave – now. But they both took my hands and led me up to the Rehabilitation Center on the third floor.

We sat in the bright waiting room filled with kids that had all kinds of different disabilities. Some were in wheelchairs because their legs weren't straight. Some of them had heads that leaned unnaturally to one side.

I felt ridiculous sitting there. I looked normal compared to everyone else. I could walk. I could talk. I could think. I didn't belong here.

When it was our turn to see the doctor, I had to do all of these crazy tests. They watched how I swallowed. They had me kick and throw a ball. I balanced on one leg and then the other. I put a puzzle together. They asked a gazillion questions about the medicines I had been taking and about the new medicine we got in Australia. They copied the research article my Mom brought about the medicine, then wanted to know about how I ate when I was a little kid. It took forever because they wanted to know every little detail about me since I was a baby.

But they didn't think I was crazy. And they didn't ask if anyone had bullied me. And they really seemed to care about me getting better. They wanted to know what kind of foods I could stand to eat, and what smells made me feel better, and what made me feel worse.

My Mom showed them all of the charts she was keeping. She showed them the chart that kept track of what I ate and drank. She showed them the weight chart we kept at home. They seemed to like the APE chart Mom kept track of that showed how my appetite, pain, and energy levels were each day. They copied her notes on the episodes of pain that I had – how long they lasted, what I was doing when I got an episode, and how bad each episode was.

At the end of the appointment, they told us that we were all doing everything we could to make me better. They didn't have any other ideas about different ways I could eat or sleep or new ways to make me more relaxed. But they did want to see me again because they said I didn't weigh enough, and I should not have the kind of pain that I did.

The next doctor we went to see was Dr. Ding. We went to Dr. Ding because my Dad had heard about how acupuncture helped a lot of people get over different kinds of pain. I wasn't too wild about having some guy stick needles everywhere on my body, but I really liked Dr. Ding. He talked to me like I was an adult. He explained how the little needles were so small they didn't hurt, but they did let the brain talk to different parts of the body. The little needles sent a message to the brain to pay attention to the place where the needle went. He told us that it might be possible to tell the brain to pay attention to my stomach so that the brain would know that my stomach was okay.

Since I was afraid of having more pain, I watched Dr. Ding put needles in my Mom first. Mom said she would have Dr. Ding help her with her migraines if I would let him try to make *Burnie* go away. I watched him put the needles in Mom, and I looked into her eyes each time a needle went in. She didn't flinch or anything. "It really doesn't hurt," she told me. So I lay down and Dr. Ding filled me up with needles from the top of my head to the bottom of my feet. The only time it hurt was if he got too close to where *Burnie* hung out in my stomach, so he avoided that area.

"You come back in a week and maybe we can get closer to your pain," he said. He also gave us bottles of vitamins Mom and I were both supposed to take. No way could I swallow the huge tablets full of dragon's claws or whatever, but lying for an hour with the needles stuck in my body was really relaxing. For a few weeks Mom would pick me up after science, and we would go take naps at Dr. Ding's with needles sticking out of us.

After three weeks Dr. Ding had some bad news. "I can't get my needles to go near where Kevin hurts." He showed me and my Mom how the needles would make big red spots if he got too close to *Burnie,* and how I would tell him the needles hurt. If the needles hurt, he would take them out right away. "If the needles won't go near the pain then there is something wrong inside that needs a different doctor than me." Dr. Ding had been a Western medicine doctor in China before coming to America to practice

Chinese medicine, so we trusted him that we needed to go back to a regular doctor.

I did keep getting massages, though. They helped me relax and made me feel better while I would lie on the table. The massage therapist that my mom brought me to did some kind of funky "energy" work on me. I didn't know what that meant, but all I had to do was lay on the massage table and relax. When she moved to one part of the room and had Mom and Dad wave their hands over me to "get my energy moving" she told them how cold that part of the room was. She seemed to think that this meant there was some kind of energy block, but I really have no idea what she was talking about. To me it just sounded like what I had heard everyone else say. "Man, there's something wrong here, I can tell, but I sure don't know what it is."

The next visit was to see an endocrinologist. By now I was feeling like I was on a weird wacky tour of the medical industry, visiting every type of specialist and learning about every kind of doctor that existed. The endocrinologist said things that made me scared. He said them in a really professional, kind way, but basically he told my parents that I wasn't getting enough to eat, and I couldn't keep living this way. He told us that with what little I was able to eat and given my low weight, I was losing my ability to grow. Apparently if I kept on doing what I was doing, I would end up basically a very short, skinny person that might never go through puberty. Or at least that's the way it sounded to me.

He told me I had to start drinking Muscle Milk and Carnation Instant Breakfast. He told my parents that if I couldn't consume 3,300 calories a day I wouldn't break the cycle of lack of nutrition that kept my growth hormones from kicking in. He told us to talk to a nutritionist and to figure out why I couldn't eat. It was rare, he said, but it appeared that for a very long time I had "failed to thrive."

So it was back to the GI doctors. And for the first time ever in my life, I saw my Mom totally and completely lose her cool. I guess it is really hard to get appointments with Pediatric GIs.

Somehow my Mom managed to get us into this one GI that everyone said was really good. I hated going to this Pediatric GI office. First, I had to go back in the hospital where there were all the bad smells, and second, we had to wait forever before we finally got in to see one of the doctors. Dad couldn't go with us to the appointment, but he and Mom had worked really hard to put together a letter to the doctor that had all of these bullet points about my symptoms and what we had tried to do to make me feel better. Now we needed to know if there were other tests that should be done to figure out what was wrong with me. The nurse at the doctor's office asked my folks to fax all of this information over to them before we went to our appointment so that the doctor would know what to do next.

I guess maybe the doctor was really busy. There were a lot of sick kids waiting to see him, and they seemed like they trusted him and liked how he was helping them. I mean, they weren't all nervous or freaked out about being there. When it was our turn to see him, the nurse spent most of the time with us. She started asking the questions that I hated. It was all about how much stress I felt about going to a new school, were the other kids mean to me, and how hard did I have to work to get good grades?

I stopped answering the questions, even though I knew I shouldn't. Mom and Dad had been telling me that the doctors needed to hear from me about what was going on. They said that if they had to keep answering for me, then the doctors thought I was weak and my parents must control my life. But when this nurse started asking the same questions that had kept me in the hospital, where right now I was sitting smelling the horrible hospital smell, the questions that I figure made the doctors put me on all of the bad medicines, I just couldn't answer. I slumped down in my chair and stared at my feet.

My Mom lost her cool. I guess she didn't like the questions any more than I did. Mom got kind of short with the nurse. She asked if she had read all of the notes that were faxed over. She asked if she had reviewed my hospital record. Then she demanded to see the doctor. The doctor came in and looked me over physically all over, in very embarrassing parts. And I lost it. Tears rolled quietly down my cheeks. His questions were just like the nurses. It was a total *déjà vu*: the smells, the questions, my body being exposed to total strangers.

"Are you done looking at Kevin?" my Mom's voice cut through my sadness. "Okay, then, he can wait in the car while we finish up." Mom handed me the keys and told me to head to the car, she would follow as soon as she finished. I don't think I had walked so fast for a year. I couldn't escape the hospital quickly enough.

Mom was shaking mad when she got back in the car. She put her arms around me and told me not to worry, she was going to figure this out. I don't know what she said to the busy doctor, but I was pretty sure I wouldn't see him again.

And I didn't see that doctor again, but I did start having lots of tests done. One day we went to a special lab in the hospital where big "Radiation" warnings were posted everywhere. I was going to be injected with a kind of radioactive liquid that would show if there was part of my belly button attached to my intestines or some kind of crazy thing. Phil came with Mom and Dad and me to this test. The guy running the lab was really nice and told me that the test didn't hurt; he just had to start an IV so the fluid could go into my blood. IVs didn't bother me at all. I showed him which vein was my best one, and he tied off my arm with a big rubber band so that my vein popped out even more.

But it did hurt. It burned so bad. I yelled for them to stop putting in the burning fluid, but it kept going in. My arm turned bright red. Phillip stopped trying to make me laugh by making crazy faces and got really quiet and sad looking. Dad's eyes filled with tears. He looked on helplessly with his hand resting on my shoulder.

And Mom told me to breathe. We had our breathing down. "In," pause for five seconds. "Out slowly," five seconds. "Fast" "*Whoo, Hee,*" in and out quickly for 10 breaths. "Hold it, hold it, nice." Then "In..." we started again. Mom says I'll be the best Lamaze coach in the world. I have no idea what she means.

I passed the Meckel's test, unfortunately. We still had no idea what was wrong with me.

Mom

Nine months into Kevin's battle, though we hadn't figured out what was wrong with Kevin yet, I began to learn the value of being vulnerable, of asking for help, of waving the white flag of surrender. When I thought I was being strong by keeping my emotions to myself and holding on to all of the responsibility for Kevin's needs, I was doing the most damage to myself, my family, even to my career. When I admitted that I wasn't strong enough to take on all that a complex chronic illness requires by myself, help showed up in the most unlikely places.

CHAPTER SEVEN

In Pain We Trust

(April 2008 – June 2008)

Whenever I brought out the camera to snap a picture, Kevin was playing around with friends, siblings and generally being a ham. Here Kevin tries on the shoes of our friend Mark Eaton. Mark is 7'4" with size 20 shoes that would swallow up the largest of kids, especially slightly built Kevin. (1999)

With a smile like this, I could not imagine that Kevin's occasional pain-filled screams suggested anything other than an earache. (1998)

I could always count on Kevin to put on a happy face and an angelic smile. Here he poses for the camera early on an Easter morning in 2000.

We assumed Kevin was just a picky eater. He would happily nibble on anything sweet. Oreo cookies were a popular, if not messy favorite. (1994)

Loving and demonstrative, Kevin snuggles up to all whom he loves. Jeff had buried a secret treasure for the kids to discover; a magical family adventure. (1999)

Kevin's picky eating habits, thin frame and occasional bouts of pain didn't curb our active life style. Here we posed for a picture during a hike to Box Canyon just outside of Ouray, Colorado. (2002)

Picture courtesy of Reg Graham

I look back on this picture and am struck by Kevin's painfully thin body. Kevin recollects this trip as the highlight of the summer before his illness began to interfere with his life. (2005)

And yet even during the trip, signs of Kevin's illness were present. What Jeff and I assumed was the beginning of an adolescent attitude was in fact an early sign of Burnie attacking Kevin's intestines.

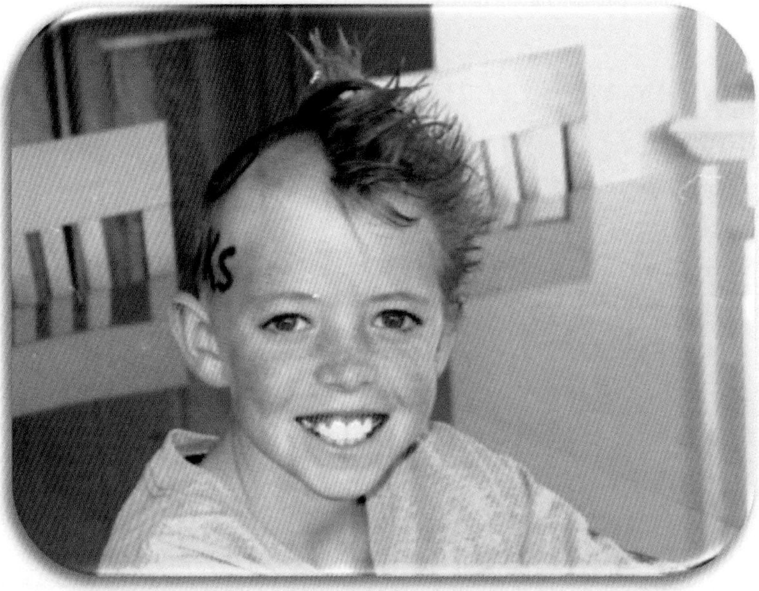

Kevin has always thrown himself enthusiastically into school, both academically and socially. During fourth grade he took crazy hair day to a whole new level. (2004)

In spite of the pain and weight loss, Kevin played soccer with all of his heart. At times we would drive to tournaments with Kevin resting in the back seat, gathering his strength for the upcoming games. Once the whistle blew to start the game he would spring into action.

Our visit with now late Coach John Wooden was magical, yet the trip home from our visit was terrifying. I am still amazed at Kevin's ability to put on a smiling face. Right after this picture Kevin retreated to another room and curled up in pain.

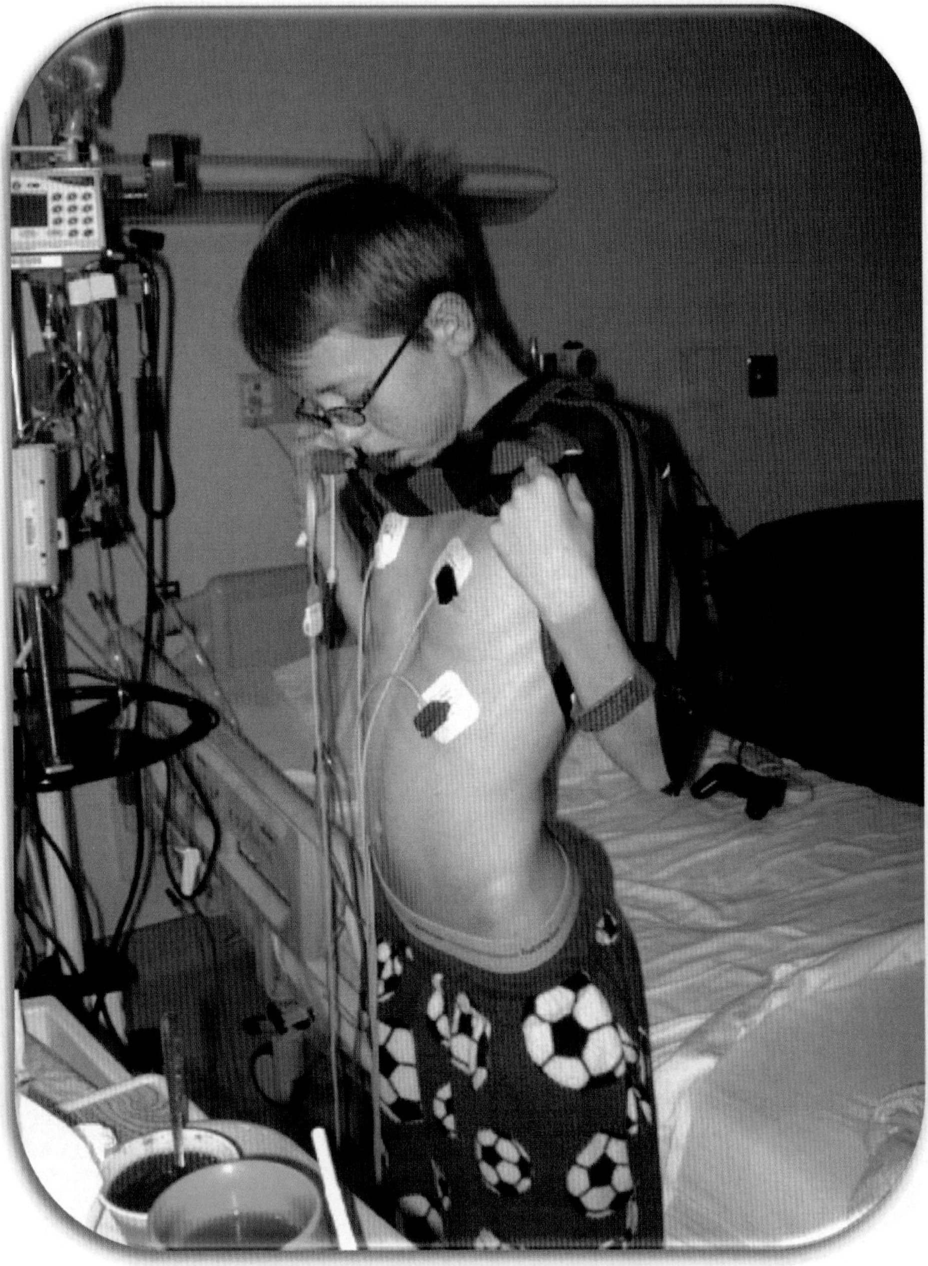

With no clear diagnosis, Kevin was admitted into the hospital to determine the cause of his pain, and to provide some much needed nutrition. Little did we know that the word 'anorexic' written to describe Kevin's thin body would be misinterpreted as 'anorexia nervosa.' The bias attached to a doctor's shorthand description of Kevin's appearance nearly cost Kevin his life.

On pain filled nights after he was released from the hospital, Kevin's bedroom would be littered with remnants of the phone books he tore up trying to distract himself from his pain. Finally asleep, a pump feeds him Ensure through his nasal-jejunal tube.

After long nights spent coaxing Kevin to hang on to life, we flew to Australia to visit doctors whose treatment plan would not be clouded by the bias of anorexia. And there were different medicines available. At the very least, a change of scenery could not hurt Kevin's spirits. In the end, the difficult journey brought hope and a new direction in how to diagnose Kevin's illness.

During the trip Kevin reengaged with life, and napped with kangaroos.

The new medicines from Australia did not cure Kevin's pain. Instead of playing with his cousins during Christmas celebrations at my parent's house, Kevin curled up with our dog, Cooie.

As winter turned to spring Kevin wanted to be out on the field playing soccer. Unfortunately, his slight frame and precarious health relegated him to the sidelines.

Patient Demographics
Patient Name: WHITING, KEVIN
Study Description: XR Sm Bowel via Enterocylsis Tb
Examination Date: 6/26/2008

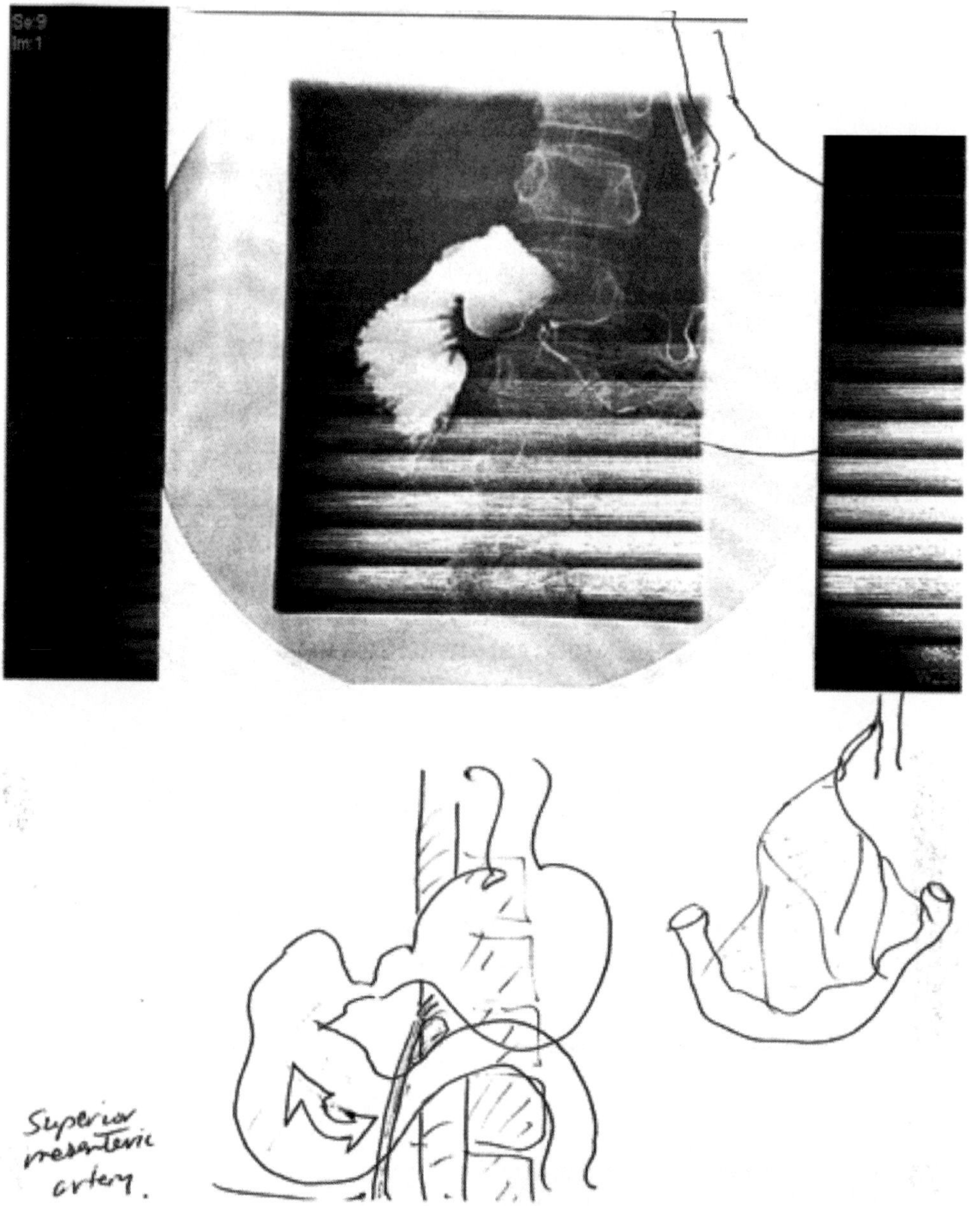

As Jeff watched, he saw barium balloon behind a blockage in Kevin's intestines. A doctor drew contrasting pictures of what Kevin's intestines looked like (left drawing). Anything Kevin consumed was blocked by his Superior Mesenteric Artery (SMA). The doctor compared the blocked intestine to what healthy intestines should look like (right drawing). We had our answer to Kevin's pain.

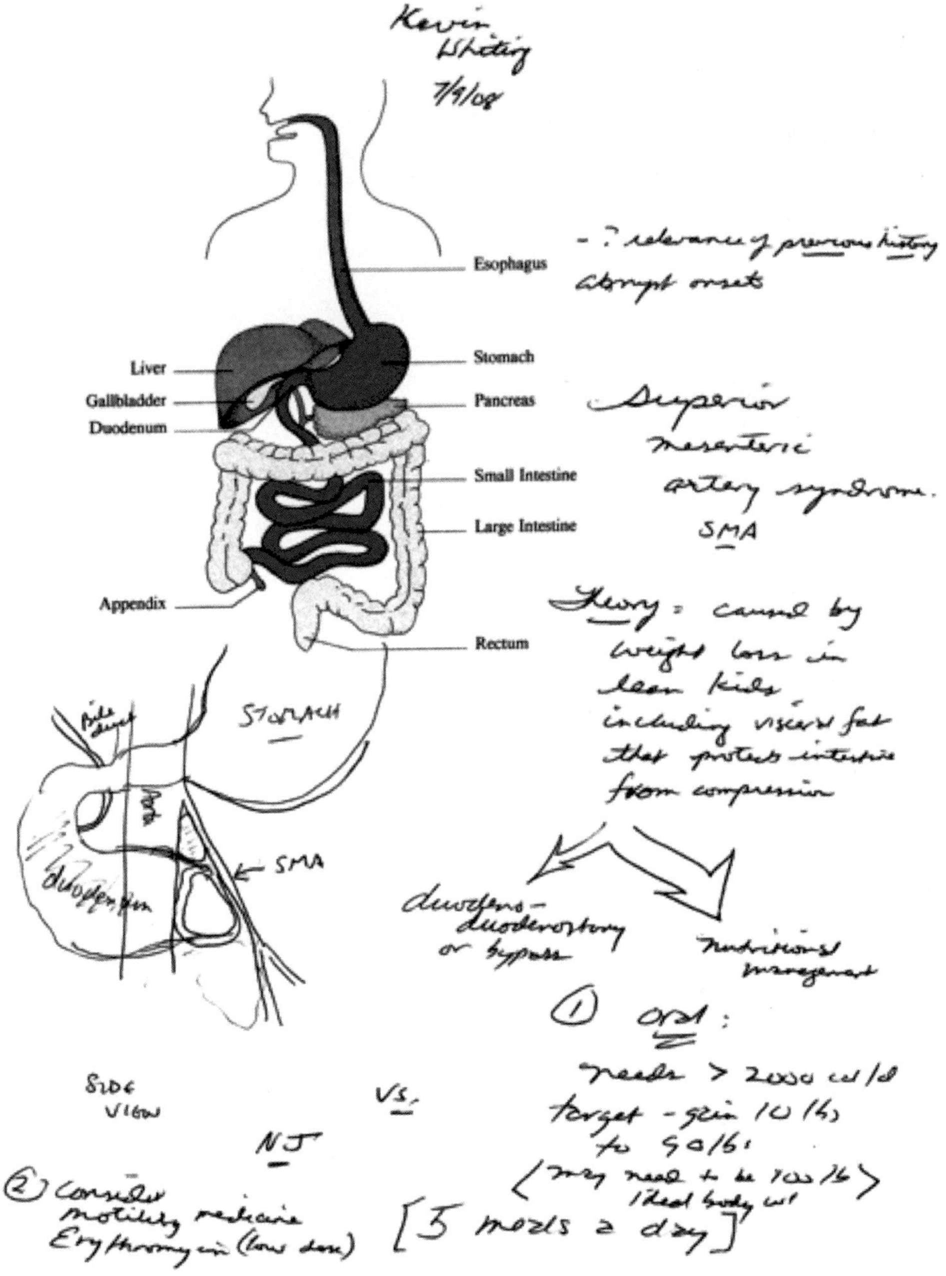

A later drawing of the cause of Kevin's pain, and how his SMA was blocking his ability to receive nutrition. The doctor's recommendation that Kevin should consume more than 2000 calories a day and gain 10 pounds missed the point that Kevin could not eat and was in constant, horrific pain.

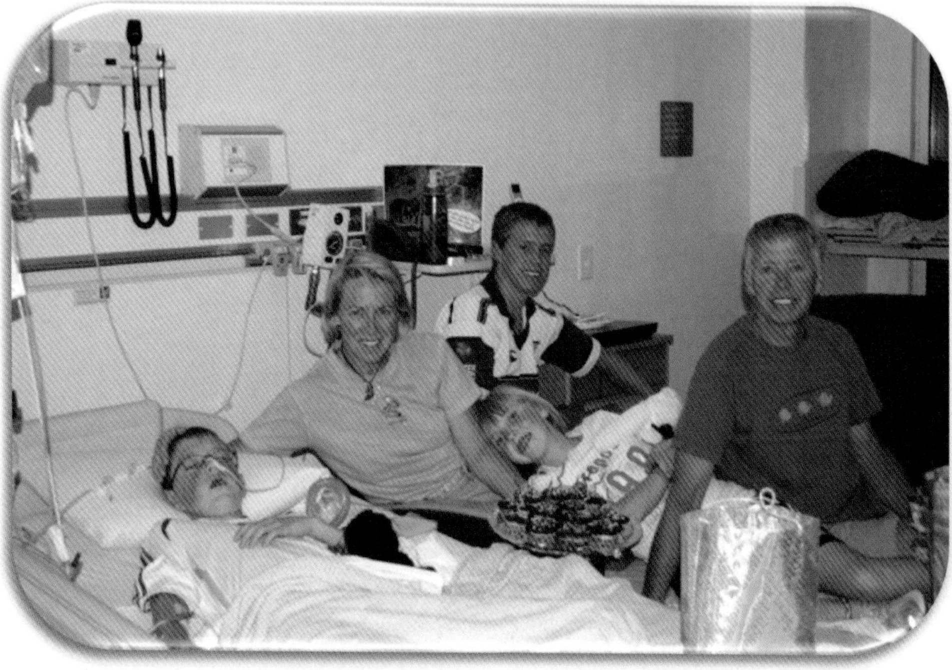

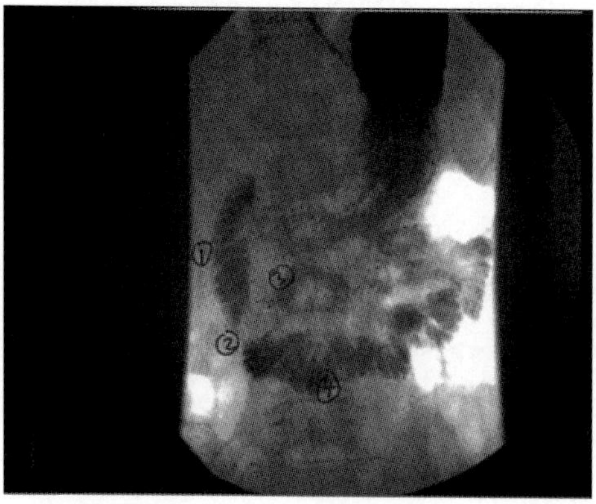

Above: We celebrate Katie's 13th birthday to the beep-beep of Kevin's heart monitor shortly after his surgery.

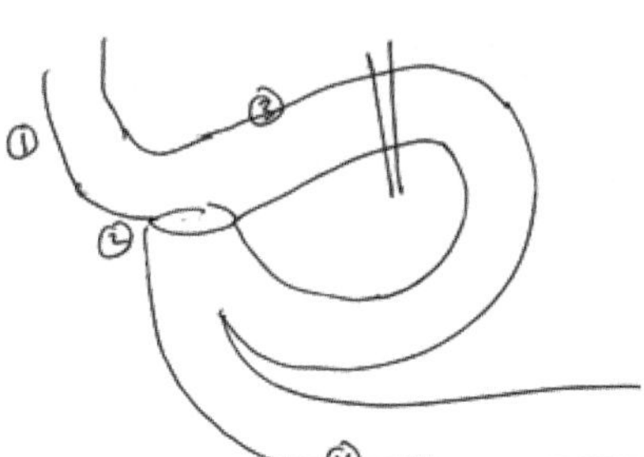

Left: A follow-up scan shows Dr. Downey's "Marbleworks" solution to Kevin's illness. The duodenojejunostomy bypassed the SMA by looping Kevin's intestines to a spot prior to the blockage. It had been ten years since this surgery had been performed on a teenager at Primary Children's Medical Center.

Kevin and Dr. Downey are all smiles when Kevin reports that he can eat bites of chicken and turkey. He will still need his PICC line for nutritional support, but now Kevin could see that the surgery had worked.

Weekly home health visits involved painful dressing changes, blood draws and worry about the stability of the PICC line.

Barack Obama's message of 'Hope' resonated with Kevin, giving him strength for the journey to be part of the historic Inauguration.

Kevin and his friend Parker Brooke share a joyful moment after Kevin shoots a perfect back of the net goal during his high school soccer match.

By the fall of 2009 Kevin was learning to live without his PICC line. Less worry meant he and Phil could play around more freely. Here Phil feeds Kevin to a replica of Burnie!

How nice it was to be able to head out of the house to enjoy time together with the family. No arm wrappings to keep the PICC line safe. No clamps to guard against blood loss. No special liquid diet. Just our family, playing and laughing together in the crisp fall air.

Christmas of 2009, Kevin's energetic spirit filled our holidays with joy.

Mom

When Kevin's pain was at its worst, he did not cry.

When he was in his worst pain, Kevin would tear phone books into little tiny pieces of confetti and scatter them about his room.

Or he would try to walk with Jeff.

Or his friend Alec or Parker would come over and play *shoot-'em-up* video games. Anything to distract him from the pain. And this is what the psychologists, psychiatrists, family doctors, and rehabilitation specialists all recommended.

But when his tears came, it was unbearable for me. They meant he was dealing with something no child should have to deal with.

The tears would come from deep in Kevin's soul. His tears would tell me that he was at the end of his ability to cope with the uncertainty. Or they would tell me he couldn't keep pushing through the pain.

Sometimes his tears were born of frustration, like the time we told him he had to drink one can of Ensure to meet the minimum number of calories to stay alive (1,200 calories).

He slammed down the Ensure like a college student drinking a beer, and then threw the empty can across the room, tears stinging his eyes.

The hardest tears I had to face, though, were the tears flowing down his face when we travelled to an "adult" hospital to have yet another upper GI test run.

For nearly 10 months we had been traveling to and from Primary Children's Medical Center. The lack of answers to what was wrong with Kevin led us to yet another medical specialist, a surgeon. And this surgeon was making things happen. He had a plan for determining what was wrong with Kevin. This plan included running barium through Kevin's intestines one more time.

The stakes were high as Kevin did his, now routine, preprocedure prep. Don't eat after 9:00 p.m., nothing to drink except a sip of water to take his medicines in the morning.

During our drive to the hospital, Kevin wanted to know if he was going to have to drink the Barium, if they were going to put in a feeding tube, and if they were going to put him to sleep.

I didn't know the answers to these questions and with honesty told him so. I repeated what Jeff and I had said to him earlier: how important it was for him to do what the doctor asked, that we needed to get the best test results, and that, no matter what happened, he had to be especially strong today.

As I walked into the X-Ray room, my heart dropped. I looked at the cups of chalky white barium lined up on the counter and knew that we were in trouble. We had been here before. The results were not pleasant.

The X-Ray technician was a pleasant young woman. She was used to dealing with adults that did as they were told, not happily perhaps, but they did what she asked.

Kevin took a look at the cups lined up for him to swallow and asked, "Do you have any raspberry flavored Barium?"

The technician realized this was not going to be her normal reluctant but agreeable adult experience. The plan was that Kevin would drink the paper cups full of Barium lined up on the counter. He had to finish them within a 10-minute period for the test to be valid. X-Rays would then be taken of his intestines every 15 minutes to track the progress of the Barium through his digestive system. Already Kevin was asking questions she had not heard before.

"Why raspberry?" the technician asked, trying to figure out if Kevin was joking with her.

"When I had this test at Primary Children's, I got to choose my flavor. I think raspberry was the best choice."

"Well, we don't have different flavors. Just hold your nose and swallow it as fast as you can. You won't even taste it."

Kevin took a deep breath. He inched over to the counter where the cups sat waiting. Gone was the valiant soldier, willing to take on whatever pain and discomfort were necessary to figure out what was wrong. In its place, there was a stooped, sad Kevin who already looked defeated.

I was worried. Without a positive attitude, I feared that Kevin would dig his heels in and fail to perform on the Upper GI test. I began cheering him on, "You can do it, Kevin… You are strong… You can handle a few swallows."

Reluctantly, after much cajoling and coaxing, Kevin brought the first cup up to his mouth. He caught a whiff of the Barium and gagged. Not a drop of Barium had passed his lips and already he was hunched over the sink, his body trying to empty an already empty stomach. The technician told us Kevin had five minutes left to drink all of the Barium; otherwise she needed the room for the next patient. I became frustrated.

"Here's the deal, Kevin, You know how hard this is going to be on me, but I'm going to have to be the bad cop. If my encouragement won't help you to drink the Barium, then maybe my threats will. Please understand that I have to do this. I don't know how else to get you to do what has to be done."

The voice in my head was telling me that Kevin's unwillingness to drink the Barium would add fuel to the theory that his inability to eat was all in his head. What if the surgeon looked at his behavior during the test and gave up on helping us figure out what was wrong? What if we went back to the surgeon's office and, after looking at Kevin's inability to consume simple (but awful tasting) Barium, there was clear evidence that Kevin did not have a physical problem, but a mental block? And so I took on the unusual but desperate role of a tough, forceful coach. I was a female version of Coach Boone in *Remember the Titans.*

"Look, Kevin, I know you have your hopes set on traveling with your friends to soccer camp." I whispered menacingly in his ear. "If you aren't strong enough to drink Barium, then I don't think you are strong enough to be on your own at a soccer camp."

I finished off the threat with a consequence. "If you don't drink the Barium, then you'll have to stay home from camp."

As a parent I knew this was ridiculous. The consequence was in no way linked to what I was asking him to do. Still, 15 minutes of sweet-talking and positive support had failed. I needed to try a different tact. Time was running out.

Shooting me daggers, Kevin picked up the first of four Barium cups. Defiantly he took four big gulps. Not even a fourth of the contents were emptied into his mouth, and immediately his body rejected the fluid.

Kevin turned to me with eyes as big as saucers. I could hear him saying, *There. Are you happy?* though no words came out of his mouth.

He tried in earnest to keep the Barium down – he hopped, walked around the X-Ray table and made a full lap before he emptied the few ounces of Barium from his stomach into the nearby sink.

I couldn't keep up the tough guy act. Not with Kevin suffering so. "What do you need to make this work, Kev-Bo-Bev," I asked, using my own special endearment to try to apologize for the meanness I had introduced into the procedure.

"I need something to take away the taste."

Of course, I thought. *He's so clever, knowing what he needs.* Begging the technician to grant us just five more minutes, I quickly ran down to the hospital gift shop. I grabbed Jolly Ranchers of every flavor, five different types of gum, and a tootsie roll for good measure.

Back in the X-Ray chamber, Kevin went back to the Barium Bar. Prepared with a wet rag in my hand, in case he vomited once more, Kevin laid out three choices of candy to mask the Barium aftertaste. Once again he steeled himself and chugged a few more ounces of Barium. Quickly he popped a Jolly Rancher in his mouth.

"*No more,*" Kevin cried.

The few ounces of Barium remained in Kev's stomach. The technician checked with the doctor. X-Rays would be taken to follow the few ounces through his system. It wasn't much to work with, but at least it was something.

This time the Barium stayed down for a full five minutes. We were told to sit out on steel-backed chairs in the hospital corridor, waiting for the Barium to progress from the stomach to the duodenum. Sitting in the hall playing Rock, Paper, Scissors to pass the time, Kevin's system once again rejected the Barium. As the technician called for someone to come clean up the mess out in the hall, the radiologist let me know that he would run the full test, but held out no hope for identifying anything with the small amount of Barium that had stayed in Kevin's system.

The drive home was a sad, depressing, confusing drive. Why wouldn't even tiny amounts of Barium stay down? I wondered. And what was causing Kevin's tears this time? Was he afraid that he had let me down? Was he afraid that no one would believe he tried his best to swallow the Barium? Was he worried that maybe the doctors were right, that it was all in his head?

Was he so tired of doctors and procedures and pain that he just needed an emotional outlet? Was he afraid that I was serious in the X-Ray room when I told him that he couldn't join his friends on their trip to the Air Force Academy Soccer Camp since he had failed to complete the Barium procedure?

Kevin

My geography class was having an end of the school year party. Even though I had been learning geography from my tutor, I really wanted be with my friends when they got to walk from school over to *Jake's* to get tacos. I knew what day they were going since I spent time texting with my friends every day.

I also wanted to go sit with my soccer team when I felt good enough to go to practice or a game. There was a doctor that told my Mom she was wrong to let me go do fun things like soccer and school parties if she wasn't making me go to school every day.

This really steamed my Mom. She went on about how this doctor was a specialist, not a parenting expert. She thought he should work on diagnosing what was wrong with me, not telling her how to be a parent during the few minutes that we were able to see him in his office.

I guess I'm lucky that Mom understood that I would do whatever I could when I was feeling up to it, whether it was to go to school or to go to practice. Maybe she didn't figure this out all by herself. I remember hearing her talk to the doctors in the rehabilitation center about whether I should be playing soccer and hanging out with friends or just focusing on going to school. They had a long talk about it and decided that I should do whatever I felt up to, whether it was school or soccer, since I liked them both. Thank heavens, since I never knew when I would feel good or bad, and when I felt good I wanted to do something other than lying on the couch, whether it was school or soccer or having friends come over to the house to hang out with me.

When I went to school, I snuck my medicine into my backpack. Mom and I knew this was against the rules, but it was the only way I would go anywhere. I needed my medicine right where I could get to it. I knew that there was no way I would share my medicine with anyone else, and I knew that no one could see me with the medicine or I would be kicked out of school. I didn't want to be kicked out of school.

Still, when a really bad attack of pain started, I could take a little Hyoscyamine pill that dissolved under my tongue, and I would get some relief right away. If I waited to go to the office and had to have the nurse give me the medicine, then the pain would take over and I wouldn't be able to function at all. Mostly, Mom and I got a routine down where I would take my pain pill before I went into school, and I had a long acting Hyoscyamine that I took in the morning and at night. It just made me feel better to know that my medicine was there with me so that I could take something right away if I needed to.

Maybe this is why I didn't really like to go over to my friends' houses at this point of my life. I just wanted to know that what I needed was close by.

My friend Parker loved coming over to my house. He couldn't believe all of the junk food that we always had on hand. Mom kept buying all kinds of treats, trying to get me to eat more calories. The endocrinologist had told her that at this point, it didn't matter what I ate, I just needed tons of calories.

Donuts were the best food I could eat. They didn't have a funny smell, they didn't make me hurt so bad and they were loaded with calories. I bet without donuts I would have shriveled up to nothing.

So, life was kinda' weird. I finally stopped taking the medicine we got in Australia. Even when we realized that it didn't fix my pain, I stayed on it for a while because it made me hungrier. I kept taking it to make me hungry.

Then we decided to see what happened if I didn't have any medicine. Mom said that we needed to get a "baseline": an idea of what was going on with my pain without any medicines confusing how *Burnie* was acting.

Burnie was the same with or without the Australia medicine. I didn't eat any more when I was taking the medicine, so I just stayed off it. All I was taking was stuff for my pain. The other medicines, the ones that were supposed to cure me, didn't make me better, and most of them made me feel worse.

So this was my life. I would wake up and take the medicine that made my pain less. After the medicine had a chance to work, I would try to go to school or to a soccer game if it was Saturday. I would see if Parker or Matt or Alec would come over to hang out with me and play video games. A lot of times they didn't want to come over because they wanted to jump on their trampoline or play with their air soft guns. I didn't have enough strength to do those things, so a lot of times I would hang out at home with Mom and Dad. We would watch *Survivor* or *American Idol* just to have something to do.

And then I would go see the next doctor that my parents had lined up. I was starting to be afraid every time I went to see a new doctor, or to have a new procedure done to me. Something different happened every time, so I never knew what to expect.

Once when I was seeing our family doctor, Dr. Rush, I told him I didn't want to keep taking my pain medicines. At school I had been told over and over that people get addicted to pain medicines, especially the kind I was taking. I didn't want to be a drug addict.

When I didn't take my medicine, I hurt so badly I couldn't eat or drink. Every time I had to ask Mom for a pain pill I felt guilty and afraid. When I didn't take the pill, *Burnie* would get so mad I couldn't do anything but lie down and curl up in a ball.

Dr. Rush helped me understand that as long as I was taking

the medicine for pain, then I wouldn't get addicted. It was when I was not having pain and still took the pills that would be bad. He also told me how the most dangerous part of the pain medicine I was taking was the Acetaminophen, not the narcotic. I guess that Acetaminophen is really hard on the liver, and I had to worry about taking too much of the other stuff that was in the pill more than the narcotic right now.

The other problem he told me about was that my body would get used to the medicine I was taking, so if I took too much, then I would need stronger pills to get any relief.

So, I still had to worry about how much medicine I was taking, but I could quit feeling guilty about it.

It had been nice not going to have procedures done for a couple of months. The massages and acupuncture and appointments with my family doctors, Dr. Rush and Dr. Dolan, weren't the horrible hospital torture sessions I hated. But, after a while, Mom and Dad figured out that the Australia medicine wasn't going to fix me. By then I was off all of the anti-depressants. My weight started to go down again, and *Burnie* stayed right with me, so then I had to go back to having procedures again.

The first procedure that I thought I was going to have in this new round of "finding out what is wrong with Kevin" was to swallow a camera. I must admit, I was pretty stoked about being able to see everything that was going on inside of me. I was scared that I wouldn't be able to swallow a camera that was like a big pill. I cut my big pills in half or in quarter to get them down as it was. So, after one doctor appointment, I was scheduled for more ultrasounds, and then I was supposed to swallow a "Pill Camera."

Getting ready for the Pill Camera seemed like standard procedure prep. No food or drink after 9:00p.m., nothing in the morning except my medicine. This wasn't hard for me since I never felt like eating anyway.

My Grammie and Papa were in town visiting. They told me how proud they were of me. They thought I was brave to handle all of these procedures without complaining.

Mom and I were driving down to the hospital when Dad called with the bad news. Instead of meeting us at the clinic where I was supposed to swallow the Pill Camera, he told us that the procedure was cancelled. Our insurance wouldn't pay for the camera. It would cost us at least $1,200. Plus, the insurance company said that this wasn't the right test for me to have.

I have no idea how any of this worked. All I knew was, the camera that was supposed to tell me if there was something terrible going on inside of me wasn't going to be used. I was crushed.

Instead, Dad told me we were going to meet with another surgeon, Dr. Eyring.

Mom

Astounded is probably the best word to describe how I felt when I got the call from Jeff telling Kevin and me to turn around and go home. There would be no Pill Camera test today. Our insurance company informed Jeff that the doctor's pre-approval request for the procedure had been denied. "How could that be?" I asked Jeff.

"I don't know, but I'm going to figure this all out and let you know what we need to do next," Jeff assured me.

This calmed me a bit. Jeff gets things done. If he was going to figure out the next step, I knew it would be a good one.

Shortly after we returned home and tried to coax some food into Kevin, Jeff called to fill me in on what he had learned.

Apparently, before paying for a Pill Camera, the insurance company requires that the patient have a colonoscopy and an

Upper GI. It seemed to me that Kevin had had an Upper GI nine months ago, but I knew nothing of a colonoscopy. In fact, a colonoscopy sounded ridiculous since Kevin's pain was up near his stomach, and he had no problems with the waste management portion of his intestines.

I railed against the insurance company to my parents. How dare they deny us the opportunity to find out what was wrong with Kevin? First the hospital, then the doctors, now this. Road blocks, nothing but road blocks.

Ironically for me, we soon found out that the insurance company was right. They were the first part of the healthcare system that pointed us to the proper diagnostics that should have been taking place all along.

By this point, we had exhausted alternative medical approaches, new medicines, altered diets, behavioral methods, diversion techniques, and doctor specialties I didn't even know existed. We'd even gone back for second opinions. Nothing shed any light on what was causing Kevin's pain. I felt caged, depressed, and afraid.

While the cancelled Pill Test was frustrating at first, in hind sight we realized that it was the tipping point that led us to a surgeon who was determined to run diagnostics, including the failed Barium Test. Jeff came home the night of the cancelled test and told me that he had set up an appointment with a well-respected colorectal surgeon. Jeff had been acquainted with Dr. Eyring for a couple of years. On occasion, Jeff would run Kevin's situation by Dr. Eyring, who would recommend specialists or medicines. It was Dr. Eyring with whom I had first spoken about my idea to have Kevin placed on medicinal marijuana. If Kevin needed to relax and have his appetite stimulated, marijuana seemed a logical prescription. I kept the thought in mind that maybe we should drive to Oregon and give it a try. Of course, I hadn't quite figured out how I would keep Kevin on the marijuana and Phillip off of it.

Dr. Eyring had better ideas. With only a day's notice, Dr. Erying fit us into his schedule. We took the last appointment of the day, not realizing the enormous sacrifice the doctor made to meet with all of us, my parents, Jeff, Kevin and me. After a long day of operating on cancer patients, the surgeon made time to talk with us for over an hour.

Because Jeff had been asking for Dr. Eyring's advice over the past 10 months, the case wasn't brand new to the surgeon. However, Kevin's symptoms did not fall within Dr. Eyring's normal practice of colon cancer and Irritable Bowel Syndrome patients. In addition, Kevin was a minor, not typical of Dr. Eyring's patient profile.

But Dr. Eyring listened.

He wanted to hear about the episodes of extreme discomfort Kevin had exhibited as a toddler. The shrieking cries of pain that occurred when Kevin would hit his growth spurts. Jeff and I would put off those cries as teething pains or carsickness; cries that my parents noted were unlike any they had witnessed in their kids or other grandchildren.

My parents explained to the surgeon that Kevin did not display the anxious or depressed tendencies suggested by other physicians, not when they compared Kevin to their other grandkids. The surgeon carefully took notes about other seemingly unassociated bits of information.

I read entries from Kevin's baby book out loud. Dr. Eyring listened when I read the entry noting my fear when, at 18-months old, Kevin would only drink water in the mornings, up to 32 ounces of water. He didn't make me feel like a bad mother when I read that at 26 months Kevin's eating habits left much to be desired. In fact, the entry noted, Kevin would live completely on sugar if it had been an option.

I told Dr. Eyring about a day in second grade when Kevin came home from school with a box of Life cereal. It had been a long time since I had thought of that day, but with Dr. Eyring's prompting, I recalled asking Mrs. Mac what had caused her to give Kevin a box of Life cereal.

"I was worried about him," Mrs. Mac explained. "For a reward when kids did well in class, I would have lunch with them. Kevin was always there for those lunches, but I noticed he wouldn't eat. Or if he ate it would only be the sweets."

Interesting, I thought. We had always considered Kevin a grazer. He wouldn't eat a full, healthy meal at home, either. I lived by an early pediatrician's words of wisdom. When I worried about Kevin's odd eating patterns, he reassured me that my job as a parent "is to put healthy food in front of your kids. Their job is to choose to eat what their bodies tell them they need." He went on to explain: "I've never seen a healthy kid starve himself to death."

I continued to explain to the surgeon that, over the years, I had become used to Kevin's odd pattern of eating. He continued to grow and be active and successful in school. I had found no reason for alarm.

Mrs. Mac, though, with hundreds of children to compare Kevin with, noticed just how unusual Kevin's eating habits were. She made it her personal mission to find a healthy alternative that Kevin would eat. At the time that Kevin brought the cereal home, I found it endearing that his teacher cared about Kevin so much that she gave him a special box of cereal. I didn't realize the importance of Mrs. Mac's discovery for a decade. And then, it was almost too late.

As Dr. Eyring collected the bits and fragments of Kevin's early life and combined them with the medical records we had been keeping for the past ten months, a pattern began to emerge. Whatever was causing Kevin's suffering had been living with him for a very long time, perhaps his entire life.

Long after the appointment with Dr. Eyring, Jeff, my parents, and I pored over Kevin's baby books. We read unusual notes I collected in the calendar that tracked Kevin's earliest years.

One entry I made struck all of us as absurd.

When Kevin was eight months old, I noted, "You are such a delightful child – very easy going. You don't complain and rarely cry. You eat when I remember to feed you and you don't seem to mind how long you go without food."

What growing, healthy child doesn't ask for food?

A contrasting entry noted, "I had to walk outside with you until 4:00 a.m. You were crying so loud I was sure you would wake everyone in the hotel. For hours we walked the streets of Ouray, Colorado. You pulled your legs up tight against your stomach. It broke my heart, there was nothing I could do to comfort you."

Finally, Jeff picked up the picture of Kevin and his siblings building a sand castle in the fog on the Oregon Coast.

Jeff and our brand new puppy stood off to the side looking on as the three kids worked intently together. Kevin's 10-year-old profile jumped out at us. His ribs and shoulder blades stuck out in sharp contrast to the curvy physiques of his older brother and younger sister.

How long had Kevin been suffering from this unnamed enemy?

Kevin

Talking to Dr. Eyring was good. He wanted to know all about what I liked to eat and what I didn't. He asked things that I hadn't really thought about, like was I ever hungry? Did I ever pig out on food before I got sick? I never really thought too much about food, but when Dr. Eyring asked me, I remembered how my friends would always eat a ton more food than me. They would eat my leftovers at lunch.

It seemed like Dr. Eyring was going to figure out what was wrong with me. He told my parents and me and my grandparents since they were there too, that there were at least eight more procedures that he wanted to have done before he would think that my problem was in my head.

The thought of eight more procedures sucked. I asked him if I could be asleep for the procedures, and he told me that if the test could be done with me sleeping, then he would see what he could do. The first procedure he ordered I had to be awake for, though. I had to swallow a boatload of Barium, and then they would take pictures of it while it went down through my intestines. I had already done tests before that made me drink Barium, and Barium isn't my favorite. The first time I had to drink Barium I did pretty good drinking as much as I could. I just sipped in a little at a time, and they had raspberry tasting Barium. It tastes like chalk with Raspberry snow-cone flavoring mixed in.

I don't know what happened when I went in to do the next Barium test. I tried my hardest to drink it, but I couldn't. When it would finally go down, I would throw it back up. It was a horrible morning. When we got home Grammie was waiting at the top of the stairs, hopeful that the first test Dr. Eyring ordered would tell us what was wrong. Grammie could tell the second that we walked in the door that it had gone badly. I just went to bed and let Mom tell Grammie how miserably I had done.

Next was a colonoscopy. I would be asleep for this test, so that was good. The bad part was that I had to clean out my intestines by taking these awful pills the night before. Worse, Mom had to teach that night, so she couldn't help me get the pills down.

Dad rented some good movies, and he set up a big beanbag type of chair in my parents' bedroom so I could get to the bathroom really fast. I started taking the pills like I was told and nothing happened. Then after awhile the pills started working, and I had to go the bathroom a lot.

Going to the bathroom a lot wasn't too bad, but taking the pills was impossible. By the time Mom got home from school I hadn't even taken half of the pills. There was a schedule I was supposed to follow with so many pills every half hour or something. But I got to a point where every time I tried to swallow one more, I would throw up. We didn't know if I should keep taking the pills or not. Finally I had taken all that I could, even though it wasn't nearly all that I should have taken. There was nothing coming out when I went to the bathroom, so Mom and Dad agreed that I had done all I could to be ready for the test.

The next day I went in for the test. I got dressed in a hospital-like gown. I joked with the nurses and Mom and Dad, and finally with Dr. Eyring. The nurses and Dr. Eyring knew every potty joke ever invented. The last thing I remember is Dr. Eyring making some joke about *Captain Underpants.*

Mom

Observing your child undergoing a colonoscopy is certainly not a comfortable experience. Yet Kevin made Jeff and I promise not to leave him. Dr. Eyring understood, but warned us that if either Jeff or I began to feel lightheaded, or if we were in the way, we would have to leave immediately. Jeff and I scrubbed up, put on hospital gowns, and followed Kevin's gurney into the darkened room where the colonoscopy would take place.

Even under anesthesia, Kevin cried out. Jeff and I remained steady on the outside, cringing on the inside, realizing that even in his drug induced sleep, Kevin still endured pain.

At the end of the procedure we shared a mixture of relief and disappointment. There were irregularities: Kevin had "Little Old Lady" intestines that drooped and might lack proper connections to hold them tight where they crossed laterally. Some sections of Kevin's intestines were unusually long, however nothing Dr. Eyring observed, that would indicate the source of Kevin's pain.

One procedure down, seven to go before we gave up hope of finding an answer.

Kevin

I know I cried when Mom and Dad told me that Dr. Eyring hadn't found anything wrong from the last test. It seems kinda' weird to be upset when nothing is wrong; it's hard to explain. See, if Dr. Eyring could find something wrong, then we could stop trying to figure out why I hurt, and start figuring out how to make me better. Also, I knew that I only had seven procedures left before Dr. Eyring told me that my pain was all in my head.

I had failed to swallow the barium during the barium test. So now I had to go through the Barium test again. I begged Mom and Dad to let me have the test done at Primary Children's Medical Center. After going to an adult hospital, I wanted to be in a hospital that makes things easier for kids, like having flavored Barium.

Dr. Eyring was worried about if I could get enough Barium in my system to make the test work. I promised I would do better this time, but I had no idea how I could keep myself from throwing up. The morning came for me to go back to Primary Children's Medical Center. I was really scared. What if I couldn't finish the test? What if they didn't find anything wrong?

I hadn't eaten all night, and I knew I wouldn't be eating again today after the Barium test. Is it just me, or does it seem weird that every week I had to spend a night and a day not eating so that the doctors could figure out what was making it so that I couldn't eat?

Mom

The car could practically drive itself to Primary Children's Center at this point. And we were pros at getting Kevin prepped for GI tests. When the doctor's office would call to confirm the preparations, I would recite the restrictions and times to the receptionist first, then ask if I had missed anything. Once or twice the receptionist would clarify my preparation summary by letting me know that for this particular preparation Kevin could actually consume clear liquids, or the end time for eating would be midnight instead of 9 p.m. Usually I was right on the mark.

I paid extra care, even on nights like tonight where the hospital didn't inform us to keep Kevin off foods and liquids. Over the past year we had so many bad memories of Kevin's being awake for difficult procedures. Jeff and I had learned the hard way that sometimes we needed to fight for Kevin to be given sedation or memory-blocking medicines. With the help of medications, Kevin was able to continue to be strong through the innumerable procedures it took to determine what was causing his pain and inability to eat.

The first time Kevin had a feeding tube inserted, he was awake for the procedure. However, the tube curled up around his vocal cords, causing him to gag, choke and finally spit out blood-covered saliva. Kevin was (understandably) upset by the time his throat stopped bleeding and the doctor was ready to try once again. At this point, I sat holding his trembling body on the X-Ray table while Jeff discussed the option of sedating Kevin so the tube could be inserted.

First, the doctor explained that it was not normal for a child to be sedated for a feeding tube insertion. We understood this, Jeff agreed, however, Kevin's case was far from usual.

After finally convincing the doctor that the only way Kevin was going to leave the hospital with a feeding tube was if he was sedated, it occurred to all of us that he couldn't be anyway. Kevin had consumed animal crackers and Gatorade within the last eight hours. The doctor could not put him under safely.

Ultimately, we left the hospital without the feeding tube, only to return the next day once Kevin had gone the appropriate number of hours without food or water. In this way, Kevin could be unconscious while the procedure was done 'with sedation'. I could avoid the heart-wrenching job of lying on top of him, forcing his arms down, while a nurse held his legs, and the doctor placed the tube up through his nose down his throat past his stomach and into his duodenum.

And so it was understandable that we all wanted to be prepared for every procedure in case the need for sedation arose. For this next Barium test, the hospital staff wasn't planning to put Kevin under anesthesia, so they didn't care whether he had eaten or not. I did. I couldn't promise Kevin that the doctor would be willing to place him under sedation and fill up his stomach with Barium via a *nasogastric* tube. I could make certain that Kevin was prepared in case sedation was an option.

As it turned out, this was a wise decision. As Kevin walked into the room where the Upper GI with Barium Contrast was to take place, he took one glance at the vat of barium prepared for the procedure and his knees buckled.

Wild-eyed, he looked first at me and then to Jeff. With the image of the first feeding tube insertion still vivid in his memory, Jeff quickly pulled the assembled staff aside and asked about sedation alternatives. The radiologist could not have been more understanding.

Whether he had been prepared to expect this by Dr. Eyring, or if he quickly picked up on the situation and Kevin's *angst*, we will never know. What we do know is that he quickly shifted gears and adjusted his busy schedule to allow Kevin to be sedated, as long as Kevin had not had food or drink since late last night.

We walked over to another part of the hospital to allow Kevin to receive the sleep-inducing medicine.

There a nurse gathered Kevin's history once again, a history we had repeated so often we were beginning to get fuzzy on the details.

Within minutes an injection port was inserted, medicine injected and Kevin relaxed into a dream world, while all around him tension mounted.

CHAPTER EIGHT

One in a Million

(July 2008 – August 2008)

Mom

Two missed calls and two new voicemails waited for me as soon as I got out of a meeting that had pulled me away from Kevin's side mid-procedure. "Please," I said a silent prayer, "let it be good news." Rather than listen to the voicemails, I called Jeff right away.

"Well?" I asked.

"They found it," Jeff answered.

Confused, I tried to process this news. Nearly 11 months had passed since we had looked for evidence that Kevin's pain was real. Now we had it.

"The radiologist called it a cascading problem," Jeff went on to explain. "It was so crazy, Vic. They put the feeding tube down into Kevin's stomach then pumped a bunch of barium through the line. The first little bit slowly slipped through, kind of like a little creek making a path on the X-Ray. Then the rest of the barium started building up like there was a dam in the middle of Kevin's abdomen. His duodenum kept getting bigger and bigger, like a water balloon filling up. I wanted to make the doctor stop. I mean, what if the intestine burst from the way it was ballooning out?"

Jeff went on to explain that as soon as the ballooning was obvious, the doctor pushed in more barium until there was enough pressure, then whoosh, the dam burst and the barium went through. When the doctor put in more barium it built up once again.

"No wonder he's hurting so bad," the doctor said. "That kind of pressure on the intestines creates an unbearable pain." The doctor remarked that it was incomprehensible how Kevin had been able to endure such an intense pain for such a prolonged time. "I can't imagine any adult putting up with this type of pain."

The doctor also explained that Kevin's condition had gotten worse the more weight he lost. The cascading problem worked like this: when Kevin was at some kind of normal height to weight ratio there were stores of fat that developed between his duodenum (small intestine) and his arteries (aortic and superior mesenteric – big strong arteries). Each time Kevin hit a growth spurt, the fat pockets would disappear and the pressure between the arteries and the intestines would restrict Kevin's ability to digest food. Kevin's ability to take in nutrition would be limited. He would eat; the food would hit the blockage, back up into his stomach, make him feel nauseated, and cause intense pain. This pain and nausea would inhibit his ability to take in food, which would make him thinner, further removing the protective fat pockets, making his situation worse.

Superior Mesenteric Artery Syndrome occurs when a patient's intestines are located too high in the branch between the aortic artery and the superior mesenteric artery, or if there is a rapid, severe weight loss such as an extended hospital stay or severe anorexia nervosa. Even in the cases of anorexia, this type of SMA, also called Wilkes Syndrome, is a rare complication. Medline explains that only 400 cases have been described since the syndrome was first identified in 1861. In fact, a miniscule amount of GI tract barium studies identify a blockage that results in a diagnosis of SMA syndrome.

Kevin had been stuck in this vicious cycle of emaciation for over a year. It's entirely possible that he had faced varying degrees of this problem his entire life.

We had our answer.

Kevin

When I woke up after the procedure, Mom and Dad showed me this picture of my intestines. It was hard to figure out what was going on. There were all these grey swirls with a bright white streak running all over the place. Then there was this huge white circle in the middle of the white streak. This was *Burnie,* they told me. The more I looked at the picture the better I understood why I felt the way that I did. I could eat and drink a little bit of stuff that would go into my stomach. Then the stomach would break down the food and send it along to my duodenum, where *Burnie* would block it off from going any further.

Mom

It's crazy the things you can make yourself believe if you want to badly enough. In the same way young children hold onto the idea of Santa Claus long after logic could explain his existence, our family held on to the belief that with this diagnosis, Kevin's troubles were nearly over. Perhaps we had watched too many television shows where, once a diagnosis is found, the cure is merely one short procedure away from fixing the patient right up. After the year we had endured, surgery seemed like an easy fix.

Jeff was doing the silly little dance he does when he's happy. He called it "the surgery dance". He shook his torso around, wiggling his shoulders in time to an imaginary drum. One little surgery and Kevin would be better than ever.

I stopped short of a celebration dance, though. Maybe I was

jaded from the year we had just survived as a family. Still, my relief at finally understanding Kevin's ailment was palpable. As for Kevin, well, he began asking every day, sometimes every hour, asking me when we would schedule the surgery that would make him well.

Kevin

Imagine the cool scar I would have once they cut me open and fixed my intestines.

That was pretty much my major thought after we met with Dr. Eyring. Nothing else mattered to me except getting the surgery as fast as possible so that I could get back to playing soccer and hanging out with my friends.

Mom

Our follow-up meeting with Dr. Eyring was soon to refocus our energy. Dr. Eyring started the appointment with an apology. *Strange,* I thought. *There is no need for him to apologize; after all, he was the one who had found the problem, not delayed the diagnosis.* He wasn't apologizing for the delay in diagnosis, though. He was apologizing up front for the significant decisions we were yet to face, the battle he already knew lay ahead.

He told us what the radiologist had found and answered the questions we had concerning Kevin's procedure. Finally Dr. Eyring let us know that he was not the best person to resolve Kevin's problem.

First of all, Kevin was a minor; Dr. Eyring was a physician

who practiced on adults. He felt strongly that the best place for Kevin to be cured was at a children's hospital. Secondly, Kevin's problem was in his small intestine. Dr. Eyring's expertise was with large intestinal problems. He did let us know that there were surgical options to fix Kevin's blockage. However, the surgery would be uncommon and technical. He was unaware of anyone having completed the procedure on a child in Salt Lake City. He recommended some websites where we could learn more about Kevin's syndrome and provided the names of surgeons he would talk to about Kevin's condition.

Our heads were spinning. Over the course of a week we had gone from elation over finally understanding what was wrong with Kevin to fear about what would be required to heal him. Off we went on another round of doctor visits, this time determining which surgeon to trust with Kevin's life.

Kevin

My friends came over to spend the night. What a blast. We slept on the trampoline until a skunk stunk us back inside. They all had to leave to go to soccer practice, but I was so tired from playing night games and having a sleepover that there was no way I could play soccer, too.

I just wanted to have the surgery and be like my friends. If the doctors had run the right tests a year earlier, I would have already been through with the surgery and back to normal.

Once the doctors told us what was wrong with me, everyone wanted to know what I thought about having such an exotic illness. They wanted to know how excited I was to get better. The phone was ringing all the time.

Talking on the phone wasn't my favorite thing to do, and telling people over and over what was going on got old. I was glad when my Mom set up a blog site at *CaringBridge.org* to fill people in on what was happening. Here was my first blog entry ever:

> *It's me, Kevin. I'm glad Mom is telling you all of the gory details cause I'm kinda' sick of them.*
>
> *It's good that they figured out what was wrong with me, but I sure wish it wasn't something so rare and hard to fix. Even though I hurt really bad every day and it is hard for me to eat I think it is easier to deal with now that I know what is wrong with me.*
>
> *It would sure be nice to know when they were going to fix me up so that I would know if I could go back to school and play a decent soccer game. Until I do, I like reading your messages to know you are thinking of me.*

Mom

What a conundrum we faced. The endocrinologist told us that Kevin needed to exercise and eat protein to get healthy. However, when Kevin exercised and ate protein, he got more pain and became very tired and couldn't digest the food he needed to consume in order to become healthy.

Kevin's days became almost manageable once we understood the nature of his illness. He learned to manage his medicine and his eating so that he could enjoy time with friends. He was even able to participate (mostly from the sidelines) on his soccer team.

Nights were a different story. The pain became unbearable and Kevin couldn't sleep. Night after night the pain would keep him awake due to his efforts to eat and build up muscle.

The cure and the cause became one and the same.

Worse, as recommended by our doctors, I looked up SMA Syndrome on the National Institute of Health website. Their entry ended with the following ominous brief paragraph:

> *Mortality: Delay in the diagnosis of SMA syndrome can result in death by malnutrition, dehydration, electrolyte abnormalities or intestinal perforation.*

Long after I would get Kevin to sleep with the help of sleeping medicines and pain medicines, I would lie awake, the NIH report echoing in my head: "Delay in diagnosis can result in death."

Surely we had dodged a bullet over the past year, but the report noted the real risk of intestinal perforation. And we now had a real picture of Kevin's intestines showing us exactly how that perforation could happen.

Kevin

I was so confused. Dr. Eyring told us that a surgery could fix what was wrong with me. I wanted the surgery worse than anything I had ever wanted in my life. Then we went back to one of the GI doctors I had seen before, and he said that I shouldn't have surgery. Worse, he told us that he had talked to the surgeons at Primary Children's Medical Center and none of them thought that I should have the surgery.

Okay, let me back up a minute – see, the exact surgery that I needed, I thought, was a *duodenojejunostomy*. It was hilarious that this is the surgery I needed. There is this one episode of *Scrubs* where Turk, the caring, nice surgeon on the show, was fighting with another surgeon, Todd (an arrogant, selfish doctor) over who got to do the duodenojejunostomy and who had to do an appendectomy.

The duodenojejunostomy was the cool surgery, and it might be the only time they would get to do the surgery. They got to do appendectomies every day, so both of them were fighting over the unusual surgery. How awesome was it that I needed the exact surgery that *Scrubs* made a big deal out of?

So, I was pretty stoked that I would get to have such a unique surgery. Then this doctor went back to saying that what I needed to do was eat more.

He drew a really elaborate picture of what my intestines looked like and where my food got stuck and why it made me hurt so bad. Then he said that what I needed to do was eat more to build up the fat around my duodenum. He listed how many calories I needed to eat and told us to meet with his nutritionist to figure out how I could get more calories into my diet.

It was like I woke up in my dad's favorite movie *Groundhog Day* where Bill Murray lives the same day over and over again. This doctor was telling me to do the exact same thing I had been trying to do for a year.

Mom

We hadn't even left the doctor's office and Jeff was on his cell phone with Dr. Eyring. Jeff was shaking mad.

My stomach had dropped to my toes. How dare this doctor look at Kevin, his pain, his weight, the picture of his intestines swollen above the point of blockage, and tell us he had already confirmed that surgeons were unwilling to fix our child?

He didn't listen to our imploring: "Kevin has tried your nutritional plan, including feeding tubes, for one year. What would make it different now that we know where his blockage is?"

He drew a picture of what was wrong with Kevin. At the bottom of the sheet he wrote:

> *Superior mesenteric artery syndrome. SMA.*
>
> *Theory = caused by weight loss in lean kids including visceral fat that protects intestines from compression.*

A small arrow pointed to the word *duodenojejunostomy* (or bypass), and the other much larger arrow pointed to the following formula:

> *1) Oral: needs > 2000 cal/day. Target – gain at least 10 pounds ([he] may need to be 100 pounds, [requiring that he gain] 20 pounds) [Eat] 5 meals a day.*
>
> *2) Consider motility medicine. Erythromycin (low dose) [an antibiotic also used for motility] vs. NJ (Nasal-Jujunal feeding tube).*

It wasn't possible. Kevin needed to gain 20 pounds to *perhaps* feel better? Yet when he had been on the feeding tube before, and his weight had increased, his pain did not subside. It did not even diminish. Why would it be different now?

Dr. Eyring calmed us. He too had talked to surgeons about Kevin's case. He reminded us that the GI consult was a requirement of the insurance companies, not a definitive course of action. Without returning to the GI specialist to confirm Kevin's diagnosis, our insurance would not pay for surgical consults.

However, Dr. Eyring assured us, there were surgeons who would give serious consideration as to whether a surgical solution was Kevin's best option. Dr. Eyring laid out a course of action for us to follow. We would contact two surgeons to get their insights into what might be done to address Kevin's illness.

Jeff contacted both surgical offices. The first surgeon that had an appointment available to see Kevin was a bit of a surprise – his specialty was gastric bypass surgeries, commonly performed on morbidly obese patients.

Kevin

Of all of the crazy days I have lived through, going to see the gastric bypass surgeon had to be the craziest of all. I felt like I had gone to sleep and woken up as Jack in the *Jack and the Beanstalk* story.

I was skinny. Not only skinny but also emaciated. Even though I was over five feet tall, I weighed less than 80 pounds.

Nobody ever teased me about how skinny I was, and I didn't think much of it until I walked into the waiting room of the gastric-bypass surgeon's office. Everything in the waiting room was HUGE! I felt like I had climbed up the beanstalk and ended up in the Giant's house.

The cushiony chairs we sat in were more like one-person love seats. Diet magazines covered every table. Even the doors we walked through were extra-wide.

On the way to the exam room there was this wheelchair. I swear our whole family could have sat in it. By the time we got to the exam room, my mom, dad, and I had a bad case of the giggles.

We were giddy at the thought that this doctor could fix me when I had the opposite problem of everyone he usually operated on. I climbed up on this gi-*normous* exam table and we waited for the doctor to come in to tell us how he could fix me.

Usually when we sat waiting for doctors we would play hangman, or the dot game where each person makes a line, trying to fill in as many boxes as you can by getting to fill in the fourth line and claim the box with your initial. While we were waiting this time we played Hangman. I stumped Mom and Dad using my best word ever: *phlegm.*

After we hung around the exam room for what seemed like forever, the doctor walked in. He had already talked to Dr. Eyring about what was going on and he had checked my history. We didn't have to tell him every single detail. He asked us really good questions, and then told us that he had done surgery on more than 7,000 people and had seen the guts of way more than that. Of all of the people this doctor had ever seen, he had only seen the way my intestines were blocked four times.

He told us that the surgery he most often performed to help overweight people could possibly help me. However, he told us, he didn't think it was the best way to fix my problem.

First, people who get the surgery have pretty bad side effects. Plus, it wasn't meant for people like me who didn't weigh enough, and he had never operated on a kid before, so he thought we should consider different ways to fix me first.

So there I was, Jack in the Beanstalk, sitting on the huge Giant's chair, afraid of what was going to happen. The doctor was like the Giant's wife in the old story, trying to help me out, but telling me that it wasn't going to be as easy as I thought.

Mom

Kevin was crushed. As much as Jeff and I had tried to prepare him for the news that this surgeon might not have the answer we were hoping for, he still held his hopes high as we went into the appointment. We were laughing and joking, holding on to the unspoken hope that there would be some straightforward fix.

Kevin was doing the math. If he had the surgery next week then he would have enough time to heal before fall soccer league started.

The doctor was superb in explaining Kevin's problem. He was compassionate and understanding. He had pictures to help us understand the challenges of the location of Kevin's blockage. Major organs drained their secretions into the section of intestine affected by Kevin's condition. Primary arteries were involved. Kevin's slight build did not leave much room for error should a problem arise.

"Well," I noted in a feeble attempt to lighten the mood, "at least it's not brain surgery."

The surgeon took on a serious tone as he explained why brain, heart, or even large intestine surgery would be less risky than Kevin's surgery.

"First," he explained, "Kevin's problem is in the nutritional end of the intestines. There are no substitutes or workarounds for long term nutrition absorption into the blood stream, especially during a teenager's growth spurt."

He continued, "Next, his blockage is located where major organ connections exist and cannot be re-routed. The secretions from these are critical for survival."

He finished, "Also, the major arteries are right there, major obstacles to work around during this type of surgery. Plus, every time you cut into intestine, you introduce nasty bacteria into the body, making the risk of an infection higher than in other types of surgeries."

Add to this Kevin's already low weight and there wasn't much cushion, should any difficulties arise.

Wow, the wind was taken out of our sails.

At the end of our appointment, Jeff asked the doctor, "What would you do if it was your child?"

The surgeon said, "I would meet with the surgeons at Primary Children's Medical Center, and trust their judgment."

Kevin

I had to wait three weeks before the next surgeon, Dr. Downey, could see me at Primary Children's Medical Center. This sucked.

There was nothing that I could eat without feeling horrid. The doctors kept telling me to drink Ensure. Yuck. I don't think these *doctors* have ever tried to live on Ensure when *they* were teenagers and all of their friends were eating pizza and cereal every day.

Seriously, what was I supposed to do? Pull out a can of this *old-people's-drink* and sit and sip on it while I hung out with my friends?

Now it didn't even look like I would have the surgery before school started. And what if this surgeon, like the other doctors, said that I couldn't have the surgery?

For a while I had been excited because I could see myself having this cool surgery and a scar to show my friends when I got back to school. I wouldn't have any more pain, I could play soccer and my life would be normal. But that's not the way it was working out. Instead I was headed back to the hospital, remembering what Dr. Eyring had said about seeing two different surgeons. I had no idea what would happen next.

After the long wait to see the next surgeon, I still had to force myself to go back to the hospital. I hate the way the hospital smells. I hate all of the bad memories that I have from there. I hated not knowing what this surgeon was going to say. The GI doctor had told us that he had already talked to the surgeons at this hospital and none of them would operate on me, which made this latest trip to the hospital seem pointless.

Mom said not to worry about it, if there was a surgery that would fix me we would fly to Cincinnati or to California or wherever we had to so that I could get well.

Once we got to the doctor's office I was surprised. The surgeon talked mostly to me, explaining to my mom (and my dad who was on the speaker phone) that I was old enough to understand what was going on and I needed to have the biggest part in what we decided we should do to get me well.

After he had asked a bunch of questions and pushed on my stomach, Dr. Downey started talking about how I needed to spend a lot more time on a feeding tube so that I could gain 20 or 30 pounds to see if that would make the pain go away. After I did that, then he would take the tube out and see if I could eat regularly and not have pain. It's hard to explain why, but when Dr. Downey told me I was going to have to do this, I knew I would do it if I had to.

I was sad when he said it for sure. I mean, this was what I had been doing for the past year and I still had so much pain. I was really afraid that I would follow his advice and in another year I would be right here in his office with nothing changed except that I would have missed another year of being with my friends and playing soccer. I would have spent another year with *Burnie* locked inside me.

And I don't know why it didn't sound mean coming from Dr. Downey like it did from other doctors. I think it's because he really listened to everything that I had to say, and he seemed to think really hard about what I was saying. And he would ask my mom questions about what I had been through then he would think some more and ask some more questions.

I guess it just felt like he was making his decision because it was best for me, not because he didn't know what else to do. Maybe the other reason is because Dr. Downey told us about a guy who had what I had that he had fixed 10 years ago. The guy now played volleyball at UCLA.

Mom

I felt as if I was watching this meeting with the doctor unfold on television in front of me. One single tear fell down Kevin's cheek. In my mind, I remembered a commercial where an Indian paddled his canoe from a crystal clear stream into an increasingly polluted river. Greying braids drooped below the Indian's proud headdress as he looked at the large city looming ahead of him, generating the pollution that surrounded him. A single tear ran down his tanned, wrinkled face.

Somehow, Kevin's face looked old and wizened like the Indian's. With that single tear streaming down his cheek, Kevin's face was hardened against the news of another year of suffering, maybe more.

And then something changed. We were nearly through the appointment. We were talking rates of nutrition to be pumped into Kevin's body, length of time needed to gain perhaps 30 pounds that would put him at a healthy weight, options for what Kevin could and could not do with his surgically implanted feeding tube (he could play soccer, he could not swim.)

We trusted Dr. Downey and the thorough consideration he had provided. He had, in the past, conducted the rare surgery recommended for this condition, so he knew the surgery as an option, but felt it wouldn't be right, given the risks and benefits surrounding Kevin's situation.

And then he asked one more question. "Why did you bring Kevin to the hospital in the first place?"

"For pain."

My thoughts went back to that plane ride, my son's excruciating pain, and to that first visit to the hospital. It seemed a lifetime ago, and surely to Kevin, it must have felt as if his life had never been normal.

Dr. Downey said to us, "If only a baseline test had been run when you first brought Kevin into the hospital, then I could know for sure."

He continued, "We'll have to be certain to get a baseline this time so we can track the effect of weight gain on the significance of the blockage."

I rummaged through my two-inch collection of hospital records, research articles, e-mails from parents whose children had suffered similar pain, calendars that tracked Kevin's appetite, pain, activities, medicines and their side effects.

Buried in the stack was a hospital record that had previously meant nothing to me, but it showed an early result. During Kevin's first stay in the hospital, our friend, who had been a pediatrician, had noted that perhaps Kevin had SMA syndrome. A test had been run at our friend's suggestion. Could this be the baseline that Dr. Downey needed?

I handed him a sheet of paper dated 10/18/2007. In the findings section of the Upper GI series, under *Impressions* there was the note: Mild delay in the passage of barium through the mid-duodenum.

Dr. Downey asked me, "How much did he weigh when this test was run?"

"Probably 65 pounds," I replied.

"So, when he gained weight on the feeding tube, what happened to his pain?" Dr. Downey wanted to know.

"It got worse," I told him, and I produced my calendar notes to show him.

"I think we need to consider a surgical option for Kevin."

Dr. Downey saw the "Zebra" that so many others had missed. The Upper GI from 10 months prior showed evidence of the existence of the possibility of SMA syndrome. Anti-depressants, pain medicines, psychological counseling, distraction from pain, reengagement into a normal routine, alternative eating approaches, feeding tube therapy, international medicines; none of these changed Kevin's outcome.

There was no time to consider how misinterpreting Kevin's test results of October 2007 had contributed to the horrific year we had spent looking for Kevin's silent killer. Instead, we looked ahead at what needed to be done to heal him.

After careful deliberation, Jeff sent an e-mail to Dr. Downey on behalf of both of us:

> *Vicki and I are leaning heavily toward the bypass surgical option. We both believe that Kevin has fought this problem since he was an infant and do not have a lot of faith that he will outgrow or gain the weight necessary to solve the problem.*
>
> *We are also very concerned with the psychological and emotional damage that is occurring and see him falling farther behind in school and in size. Your thoughts and comments are appreciated here.*
>
> *We have put a hold on a surgery date with your nurse. This may be premature, but your nurse advised us to do so given your schedule and perceived urgency of the situation. We both feel very comfortable with you and have confidence that you will help us to make the best decision possible.*
>
> *Nothing is certain but we feel with your guidance we can choose a course of action that we can all feel good about.*

Dr. Downey replied:

> *I agree with your leanings toward the bypass operation.*

The nutritional approach with the tube, etc. would be more amenable to an acute situation, which Kevin is not. In addition, some surgeons claim a non-bypass operation is successful, but I do not think this is a good choice; it is unpredictable and has a significant rate of failure.

The bypass [success rate] is 90% and I think the 10% is mostly in older and more debilitated patients.

I agree with you that the chronicity of this problem dictates that nutritional management will improve but not cure him.

The surgery would be difficult, Dr. Downey noted. We needed to be prepared to "tough it out" once the surgery was complete, for Kevin's intestines might not work right away.

I am concerned that he may take some time recovering from this operation. Even though the bypass is successful and the obstruction relieved, the area upstream from the obstruction is chronically distended and will take awhile to function normally. Hard to predict this and he will likely still need some outside nutritional support recovering.

Even with this foreshadowing, there was no way for anyone to predict just how hard "toughing it out" would be, and how many long, frightening months we would have to endure to find out whether Kevin's intestines would ever work again.

CHAPTER NINE

Bye Bye, Burnie

(September 2008)

Kevin

I don't remember much about the weeks I was in the hospital after my surgery; only a lot of pain, a lot of nausea, a bit of throwing up, and a lot of TV.

One day it was sunny and warm and I was outside playing air soft games with my friends, and the next I was tied to a hospital bed with all of these tubes coming out of me.

The day that I had my surgery was the same day that my brother, sister, and all my friends went back to school after summer vacation. When we were playing Sunday afternoon, all my friends kept telling me how lucky I was that I didn't have to go back to school. They had no clue. To me, school would have been awesome. I didn't tell them, though. I don't think they could understand.

My sister got it. She was really sad for me. When she started packing up her backpack with all of her new school supplies, she came up to me and gave me a hug.

While she and Phillip got all their stuff ready for school, I had to go down to the hospital to have blood taken out. They were running these tests to know what all of my different blood levels were so they could track them after my surgery. They took out extra blood in case there were any problems so I could be fixed with my own blood instead of blood from a stranger.

My excitement about getting fixed by surgery was gone. Now I was nervous.

Mom

Monday, August 25th. We didn't need to write this down on our calendar. As soon as Dr. Downey scheduled us in for surgery, the day was branded in our minds.

"Toughing it out until his intestines worked." That's what Dr. Downey said we needed to be prepared for.

Two to four weeks' recovery time, he thought, though it was entirely based on how much damage Kevin's intestines had sustained in the months and years prior to diagnosing his illness.

And so we prepared ourselves as best we could. We made calls to family and friends, updated *CaringBridge.org*, and sent e-mails to let people know they could check in anytime to stay informed.

Prayer chains started in churches, synagogues and mosques. Our eclectic group of friends gave us access to many paths of blessings. While Methodists, Presbyterians, Catholics, Episcopalians, Jews, Lutherans, Mormons, Unitarians, Baha'i's, Buddhists and Muslims prayed and offered blessings, our agnostic and atheist friends held Kevin in their thoughts.

A colleague used *HelpingHands.org* as a platform to coordinate support for us. Meals would be delivered both to the hospital and to our house. People offered to take over carpool commitments and to help run errands. My parents were set to arrive once again to hold down the house and help with Phillip and Katie. Jeff and I would shuffle between home and hospital.

We were incredibly blessed to have so much support.

Anyone who has kissed their child "goodbye" as they lay on a gurney, small and pale against the hospital's white sheets, understands how the heart skips a beat during the final lingering touch.

Saying goodbye to Kevin asleep on that gurney twisted my heart. Jeff held gently to Kevin's right hand, I held his left, an IV bag dangled behind us as we clung for as long as possible. Then the double doors to the surgical suite opened, and Kevin was ushered through.

All day Jeff and I attempted to distract ourselves, waiting anxiously for each intermittent report from the surgical suite. We were paged while at the cafeteria, a nurse informing us that Kevin was holding steady during the surgery.

Another page came hours later. This time Dr. Downey was calling. "It was the right decision to choose surgery," he said. "Kevin's intestines are severely atrophic. This means that he has suffered from the blockage for quite a long time. It means that healing from the surgery is going to be a tough battle. Without surgery his body never would have worked right."

The next page sounded: Dr. Downey's work rerouting Kevin's intestines was complete. A second surgical procedure to place a Peripherally Inserted Central Catheter (PICC line) for intravenous eating and medicine delivery was underway.

And the final page arrived. One parent was allowed to join Kevin in recovery. Thank God.

By 7:00 that evening Kevin was set up in his new hospital room. Tubes and cables protruded from Kevin's nose, arm, chest and feet. A thick nasogastric tube snaked out of Kevin's nose. Several times each minute a machine suctioned the brownish fluids which backfilled into his stomach from Kevin's non-functioning intestines up through the tube into a jar attached to the wall behind his head.

The IV running through Kevin's veins had a double port – one for fluid nutrition and another for medicine. Around Kevin's face rested a clear plastic line, providing additional oxygen. His big toe was enveloped in an oxygen saturation meter, his bicep gripped by a blood pressure band that inflated at regular intervals. Pads attached to Kevin's chest sent data to a heart monitor screen over his head. A personal administered pain (PAC) medication pump monitored the flow of morphine he received.

Somewhere under all of the tubes and cables, housed in a special sterile wing of the hospital, Kevin was safe. Kevin was on the path to a new life -- free from pain, able to grow.

Kevin

Every time I would wake up I'd remember that I was still in the hospital. I had tubes running out of my nose and my arm. Wires stuck out of my chest and off my toe. I couldn't move my body and it was hard to swallow. I couldn't eat or drink anything. I hurt so bad. Not the old *Burnie* pain, but a different type of pain, a kind of tearing feeling that got really bad if I tried to raise the hospital bed or take a deep breath.

I'd wake up enough to make sure someone from my family was beside me. Sometimes it would be my sister if my parents had to work. Or sometimes it would be my Grammie and Papa. Usually it was my Mom or Dad. As soon as I knew I wasn't alone, I would touch the morphine button, then I would go back to sleep.

Mom

Days at the hospital were a strange mix of calmness and intensity. While it had been explained to us that Kevin would struggle, we had no idea what Dr. Downey meant when he told us we would need to "tough it out."

Each day Kevin was exhausted and sedated. Pain management teams arrived twice a day to make sure that the morphine drip allowed Kevin to rest. I measured the amount and color of the fluids pumping out of Kevin's stomach. Dr. Downey explained that normally the secretions turned from a dark brown to a lighter color as less blood entered the intestinal tract. The amount of fluids should decrease signaling that Kevin's intestines were processing the secretions rather than the fluids backing up into his stomach.

Anxiously, we waited for the bile to lighten in color, for the amount of fluid to decrease, for Kevin to be able to get out of bed, and for the go-ahead that Kevin could attempt to sip some fluids. As days turned into a week a doctor counseled us to use a calendar, not a clock in situations like this. Otherwise, he explained, we would drive ourselves crazy waiting for signs of Kevin's healing.

Each evening a crowd would filter into Kevin's room. First Katie would arrive after school with my parents. Next, Jeff would rush over after work. Phillip would arrive after his soccer practice. Often friends would bring dinner by the hospital for us and they would check in to see how we were holding up. Jeff and I helped Katie and Phillip with their homework. Grammie and Papa read the paper.

In the background, analysis of the presidential primaries filtered into the room. It was the September before the 2008 presidential election. Primary party nominations were in full swing. Democrats Hilary Clinton and Barack Obama were in a tight race, with the decision yet to be made by party delegates. The Republicans had decided that John McCain would be their delegate, though much news analysis centered upon whom he would choose as his running mate. As Kevin snoozed, tethered to his hospital bed, every television channel ran non-stop election coverage. We would hold Kevin's hand as he slept, one set of pumps sending fluids into his body, another pulling the fluids out. Around us the world was captivated by an election that, regardless of its outcome, would be historic.

Kevin's room took on a cozy ambience. A special "Soccer 24/7" pillowcase cradled his head. Stuffed animals sat next to him. An entire wall was covered with get-well cards. Cards from classmates, soccer buddies, teachers, friends around the world, and even from strangers who had heard of Kevin's plight were taped up as reminders of the loving support that existed.

We hauled thick quilts and cozy blankets from home. These softened the recliner next to Kevin's hospital bed for more comfortable nighttime sleeping. Portable speakers provided familiar music and helium balloons gave the room a cheery feeling.

Katie's 13th birthday arrived during Kevin's hospital stay, so we hosted a party in the room. Katie wrote her take on the hospital birthday scene.

> *Beep. Beep. Beep.*
>
> The heart rate machine is on beat the whole time. I find myself here most days after school as the doctors try and try to figure out how to fix my brother. He is asleep out of exhaustion most days.
>
> All I can see of the brother that used to be the most active in our family is his struggle to stay alive. I can't stand seeing him in pain, so I escape to the cafeteria.
>
> When I come back, Kevin barely opens one eye and tells me, "Happy Birthday, Katie," then he falls right back to sleep. I tried to put aside the fact that I was spending my birthday in the hospital with Mom and Dad, who were too worried about my brother to show me the affection that I was hoping for.
>
> My neighbors, the Botkins, and my teacher, Ms. Hooker, worked hard to bring me a happy birthday. They brought me balloons at school and cupcakes to eat during my hospital party.
>
> Mostly I sit in a chair that I stole from the nurses' station and stroke the fur on my new teddy bear's soft head.

We have to leave my Mom and my brother at 9:00. As I go to leave I give my brother a hug. I can see his rib cage poke out of his scrawny body, and I honestly can't see how he is still alive after the last year.

Before I go to sleep my Dad tucks me in and gives me a beautiful stone necklace I had admired when we went to the Jazz Festival. I hold on to the necklace wishing instead that I could have my family together at home and healthy for my birthday present.

One week dragged into the next. Medical teams would silently appear at 6:00 a.m., hunched around the medical records tracking the progress of Kevin's rerouted intestines. The team of doctors and nurses would check incision wounds and the color and amount of bile pumping out of Kevin's stomach.

I would awaken from my restless sleep to ask what they thought. Would today be the day that Kevin could try to take liquids by mouth? Never sure, they deferred their answers to Dr. Downey who would be arriving later in the day.

We waited for the time when Kevin could test out his new intestines with a sip of Gatorade.

Kevin

A cool golden retriever therapy dog came to visit me in the hospital once I got to stay awake longer. Gizmo made me miss my dog Cooie so much. Gizmo was the reason I got out of my hospital bed. It hurt so bad to move that I wanted to just lie as still as possible, but Gizmo would look at me with her pleading brown eyes and I would think, well, it will make Gizmo happy if I get out of bed and walk a few steps with her.

When Gizmo would come to visit, I would walk further with

her than I ever had since my surgery. After a little while, we even made it down the hall and around the corner before I was too tired to walk anymore.

Even though I could walk, I had a wheelchair to get around. I needed to use the wheelchair to get around until I was strong again. That way I saved my strength and I didn't burn as many calories. Phillip liked my wheelchair way more than I did. He could balance on the back wheels for at least five minutes. Show off.

Mom

After a week and a half, Kevin became alert enough to feel the torture he was enduring. His sense of smell came back, and with it nausea from the smells of food brought into his room. He would awake from dreams of sipping sweet Tampico juice, his chapped lips and dry, gummy mouth begging for relief from the dryness. A small relief came in the form of little wet pink sponges, stuck on the end of a lollipop stick, Vaseline put on his lips, and a few ice chips to wet his mouth. Nausea from backed-up bile became Kevin's constant companion. Reglan and Zofran, anti-nausea medicines, became staple medicines injected into his IV port.

We arranged for his friends to come for a visit, hoping their presence would take Kevin's mind off of his discomfort. It was awkward, not like past hospital visits where friends offered a distraction from the monotony of procedures and uncertainty. This time Kevin asked us if we could tell his friends not to visit. He didn't feel well enough to interact with them.

Twice a day a medical team came in to conduct *down drain* procedures to test Kevin's intestines. They checked to see if his stomach bile moved down and out through his intestines rather than back and up into his stomach when the pump sucking out the bile was turned off.

Nine long days it took for Kevin's intestines to allow the enzymes created by his pancreas, gall bladder, and stomach to move down through the labyrinth of his intestines.

Finally, the stomach tubes were pulled out of Kevin's nose. The stomach pump turned off.

Kevin

I thought I'd be happy about getting the tubes pulled out of my stomach. And I was, don't get me wrong, but just having the tubes out didn't mean that I could eat and drink anything. I was still really nauseated and my guts still hurt really badly from being all sliced to bits.

I knew the surgery had worked, which was great. *Burnie* was gone. Now I had a different kind of pain. The kind you get when your intestines are sliced open at four different places, then the surgeon builds these new pathways for your food to go through.

Picture the kids' game *Marbleworks* where you can design different routes for the marbles to go down. That's what my intestines looked like now. There was a path going the regular way, then another path that looped around a different way. The only problem was that the regular way didn't work because it had been broken for so long. And the new way didn't work yet because it had just been built and my body didn't know how to use it or something.

Mom

As each tube and peripheral was removed from Kevin's body, he became more responsive. After nearly two weeks, I added this entry into the *CaringBridge.org* blog that served as our link to the outside world:

> *Kevin smiled today. It lit up the room. When we were talking we decided that he was living in a season-long television show, a lot like "Man vs. Wild".*

Kevin wrote the following on our *Caringbridge.org* blog:

> *I am Man.*
>
> *Wilkes Syndrome is Wild.*
>
> *The family, meal makers, gift card providers, card senders, grass mowers and all of the other people who are helping me out right now are our production crew.*
>
> *Everyone is really important to help me get well. The only problem is that I WANT OUT OF MY CONTRACT.*
>
> *I didn't apply for the role and I am tired of being the star of the show. Like the tough guy on Man vs. Wild, I try really hard not to complain. I don't think that I have been a whiner.*
>
> *Since I've been stuck out in the wilderness, with Wild creating all kinds of threats for me, I haven't gotten any commercial breaks. I don't even know when the season will end.*
>
> *I do know this; I am ready for the season to be over.*

Closing in on two weeks it became clear to everyone that Kevin's intestines were not springing back to life. Doctors and nurses began talking about the necessity of Kevin going home with his central catheter (PICC line) in place. Kevin was unable to eat or drink. In order to survive, Kevin's life depended on fluid nutrition flowing directly into the major artery just above his heart.

For the past two weeks I had observed the care nurses took when changing IV bags of fluid nutrition. They had explained to me the risks associated with a central line. They had convinced me of the importance of taking extreme care when dealing with any part of Kevin's catheter.

I watched as they cleaned the site of Kevin's surgically implanted central catheter. I held Kevin's hand during painful dressing changes. And I felt relieved that these compassionate, well-trained professionals were in charge of the pumps, alarms and equipment needed to sustain Kevin's life.

Now it became obvious to the medical staff and to me that I needed to learn how to take on these responsibilities. Kevin would be coming home with his PICC line. Rather than standing curiously to the side during Kevin's nursing care, I became an active participant. During the final day of Kevin's preparations to return home, I checked Kevin's catheter insertion point. Kevin had been complaining about pain at the site, and I passed this information along to the IV team.

A quick look at Kevin's arm told them everything they needed to know. Kevin's arm had developed a dangerous blood clot. Kevin needed to undergo one more surgery to reinsert his PICC line. Fortunately, this occurred right before we had checked out of the hospital. Professionals quickly recognized and corrected the problem. I'm not certain I would have caught the problem at home.

Seeing first hand how quickly a PICC line could become a dangerous health risk infused me with terror. At home it would be up to me to manage all aspects of Kevin's healthcare.

Kevin

It sucked. I was supposed to go home. I was supposed to be done with surgeries. Instead a stupid scab of blood clogged the vein that let me eat through my IV tube. So I had to stay longer in the hospital. And they had no idea how long I might have to be on this IV. Maybe months, I heard the doctors say.

I did get to take some sips of orange Gatorade before my arm got messed up, and it tasted really good. Every night the only thing on television was the presidential election. One of the last nights I was in the hospital there was a big speech in Chicago. Barack Obama accepted the Democrats' nomination for him to run for president. I'll always remember that speech. He stood in front of hundreds of thousands of people and told them about *Hope.*

Burnie, the painful guy who had lived in my intestines making my stomach burn so bad was gone. But in his place was a bunch of this other pain. And I couldn't eat or drink anything.

This wasn't at all the way I had pictured it.

After everything I had been through, now I had to go home still hooked up to an IV so I could "eat." I was in so much pain that I needed pain medicine all the time. I was feeling pretty low. That's why I really liked what Obama was saying about Hope. I needed Hope really bad right now. I kept hoping that my intestines would start working.

After everyone was sure my new PICC line was working I got to go home. Mom and Dad set up a bed downstairs on the couch for me. My upstairs bedroom was more like a hospital room with the IV pump and all of my medicines and bandages and my wheel chair and everything. Every time I would wake up, I'd think at first that I was still in the hospital. I thought that I still had tubes running out of my nose, and I still couldn't eat or drink anything.

I would wake up, look around and see that I was home. I would know that I was safe, think about *Hope*, then go back to sleep.

Mom

I thought I'd be happy to get Kevin home from the hospital. Instead I was a nervous wreck. The afternoon he came home was a parade of home health professionals. First, the infusion specialists arrived with a three-day supply of Kevin's specially developed 'Total Parenteral Nutrition' (TPN). Every two or three days a pharmacist made up a special mixture of lipids, proteins, vitamins and minerals adjusted to Kevin's most recent blood counts. These vacuum packed bags of liquid would be delivered to our house packed in ice to keep the nutrition stable and bacteria at bay.

Next, the medical equipment specialist arrived with a wheel chair and IV peripheral. Finally, the home healthcare supervisor arrived to train Jeff and me on the intricacies of Kevin's central line management. We were taught how to inject vitamins and minerals, instructed in the importance of slowly allowing the TPN to adjust to room temperature prior to feeding it into Kevin's veins. We were coached on how to attach and detach Kevin's port, bleed the air out of the feeding line and program the pump settings. Warnings were given about air bubbles, infections, occlusions, and pump maintenance.

We were given a three ring binder to manage Kevin's care, along with numerous phone numbers to call in case of emergency.

Kevin's first night home I lay awake all night listening for the reassuring sound of the wheel turning to pump nutrition deliberately through Kevin's arteries.

Kevin

In case you are wondering, it takes three hours to get ready to eat if you are eating out of an IV.

First you have to inject vitamins and medicines into the food bag, and then let the food get to room temperature, or else the cold liquid hitting your heart can give you a heart attack.

Then you have to really carefully clean off the port that will hook up to the bag of IV food.

Next, once the food is warmed up to about room temperature you have to prime the line. This means that you have to get all of the air bubbles out of the line. Air bubbles are bad things if you send them right into the artery above your heart, so you have to slowly get all of the air out of the IV line without letting the end of the line touch anything because then you could catch a virus or something when you connect the IV to the vein line. Putting a virus into your vein is bad. You have to flush the line with saline before you eat, then with saline and heparin after you eat. This keeps the blood flowing smoothly.

After all of this is done, you can finally hook the bag up to the IV port and start to eat.

While you are eating from the line you have to be careful that there are no kinks in the line, which is hard since you are trying to sleep and the line moves with you when you turn over or anything. The pump squeals if the line gets crimped -- that's called an *occlusion.* The pump also squeals if there is any air in the line, which sometimes happens because there is sometimes a little bit of air in the food bag. If you run out of battery power the pump screams as well.

Man, that was one *screaming* pump!

My first pump got to the point where it screamed every night a bunch of times. Finally, Mom called the pharmacist that made up my food everyday and he said that shouldn't be happening. He sent a new pump out the very next day and the next pump worked way better. Then I could get more sleep.

Mom

After a couple weeks of recovering at home, Kevin felt well enough to start getting out of the house. Once he was ready to return to school on a part-time basis, we began a routine that would carry us through spring. We tried to get Kevin's TPN flowing by 8:00 each evening. In this way, I could get him unhooked after Phillip left the house at 7:00 a.m., but before Katie caught the bus at 8:30. If the IV was not disconnected at the right time, I was afraid that the pump might continue to run with nothing in the line.

After getting Katie off to school, I would focus my attention on Kevin. He would be tired in the morning, and his pain was most significant then. I figured the muscles in his gut stiffened up over the night and they took awhile to get loosened up in the morning. If Kevin took a shower, he needed help to carefully protect his PICC line dressing. Water was a big risk for bacteria and possible infection.

Each day I drove Kevin to and from school for one or two classes. Since Kevin's school had a modified block, Kevin would take English one day, and Science the next. Often we also needed to drive to appointments, and I did my best to encourage Kevin to drop in on soccer practice or to join me at the grocery store. As tiring and painful as it was for Kevin to move about, I felt like it was important to get him out as much as possible.

As we drove, we kept the radio tuned to the station POTUS, which, of course, was named after the president's nickname "POTUS" for *President of the United States.* Election day was nearing, and Kevin seemed drawn to the election speeches. Sometimes I would change the station to music, but then Kevin would always ask me to change back to POTUS.

In the hospital the Democratic and Republican conventions had played out as a backdrop to Kevin's recovery. As the months wore on and the election came down to Barack Obama and John McCain, Kevin wanted to listen to their speeches. As Obama spoke about *Hope* and *Change*, Kevin took the words to heart.

Too young to understand the complexities of the political platforms, Kevin knew better than most the importance of *Hope.* For a year he had clung to the hope that the cause of his pain would be identified. His next hope was that the surgery would cure his problem. Now he lived with the hope that his intestines would begin working, and he would not be sentenced to a life lived on a surgically implanted feeding tube.

Kevin

I started going back to school a little bit. Mostly I learned at home with Sue as my tutor again for another year. I couldn't believe that soccer season was almost over. I love the fall soccer league. All of my friends play on the team. After the games we sometimes go out for pizza, then on the days we don't have practice, a bunch of us hang out together.

Before my surgery I had figured that I'd be back with the team by the end of the season. Now it was October and all I had been able to do was watch part of one game sitting on the sidelines in a wheelchair. I thought it would be fun to see all my friends and to watch them play, but it ended up being really hard not being part of their fun.

When I got out of the hospital after my surgery, I really wanted to go see all of my friends from soccer. They had a home game, so I decided I would go sit on the bench with my buddies on the sideline. My Mom and Dad helped me into my wheelchair to watch my friends play. They pushed me down to the field. I tried to wheel myself across the grass so I could sit with the team, but man is it hard to push a wheelchair through the grass. Real quick my friends on the team jumped up from the bench and pushed me the rest of the way so I could sit with them.

After being in the hospital for so long I kinda' thought that seeing my friends would be the best thing ever. But it wasn't. It was sad. They were all focused on the game.

I was freezing cold even though it was a warm fall day and I still had a bunch of pain from the surgery. After the game, my friends were talking about stuff I wasn't part of. It made me sad that I wasn't really in their gang anymore. I hoped that I'd be able to eat and play and get back to school fast so that I could be around my friends again.

Mom

In a blink it was October. Fall was flying past. Seven weeks into post-surgery we had a new routine. Kevin was covering the four subjects necessary to advance to the 10th grade by attending one class a day and working with his tutor, Sue. Most of Kevin's life was spent hooked up to his IV, though. He didn't have much energy and still had pain from the major surgery his body had endured.

The excitement mounted when he had his first real outing in nearly two months. Bundled in multiple layers of clothes with pocket warmers and his wheelchair, Jeff and Kevin joined his friend Parker and his dad for a boys' night out at a *Real Salt Lake* soccer game. Kevin came home tired, but happy. It had been a great time, he said.

Parker's TPN was all ready for him when he got home. Still not eating, Kevin felt his body demanding the nutrition provided through his arteries. It was hours past his normal hook up time. When I went to hook up his "dinner", however, blood began backfilling the IV port. Something was horribly wrong. Instead of nutrition flowing from the IV into him, the pump was pulling Kevin's blood out of his body. Quickly we shut down the pump, cleared the line with saline and heparin and called the doctor.

Kevin's skin and his port had given out. He would have to get to the hospital first thing the next morning to have a new PICC line inserted. Sadly, Kevin checked back into a room on his old hospital floor for the insertion of his third PICC line. He got to see a few of his former nurses. While they liked seeing him, they weren't at all happy about his return.

It had been two months of "toughing it out", waiting for Kevin's intestines to work. We had psyched ourselves up for two to four weeks of waiting for Kevin's digestive system to begin working. We held on for the next six weeks. Now we were staring the two-month marker in the face with no end in sight.

Days and nights were a blur of medical procedures and fear. Alarms sounded, waking me, waking Kevin, waking Jeff as we cleared kinks in the line, bled off dangerous air bubbles, replaced batteries, and soothed Kevin's jangled nerves. At the two month point Kevin still could not eat without the food coming up instead of going down. He lived in a state of nausea, barely contained by anti-nausea medicines. His muscles cramped painfully at night, whether from lack of use or growth pains, we will never know. Abdominal pain was less severe but ever present. Surgery to remove his pain had created a new form of pain and nausea, and a new level of uncertainty. Would Kevin's intestines ever function?

Kevin's spirits crashed. Jeff and I were exhausted from waking up through the night every night to keep the pump running. Kevin's 15-hour medical ritual kept the entire family tethered to the house. No one was having fun.

At his post-surgical appointment, Dr. Downey reminded Kevin (and thus Jeff and me) that because he was still nauseated and had no appetite, his intestines still were not working. No one knew how long it would take for his intestines to work. However, Dr. Downey was not giving up hope that they would eventually begin to work. He reminded us that Kevin was a very sick young man, and that what he had seen of Kevin's intestines during the surgery indicated that they were so incredibly stretched out, it could very well take them many months to work.

Kevin

I got tired of spending 15 hours a day dealing with a central line. I dreaded the nurses coming to change my dressing. One time my PICC line got stuck to the tape during a weekly swap of my bandages and my PICC line pulled out of my body almost an inch. I was so scared that I would have to go back in to have another line put in. I felt terrible for my nurse. She was so worried that she had messed up my line. It wasn't her fault, though. She was being really careful. It just happened. Lucky for me my line worked its way back into the right place, and I could go on just hooking my food up to the port each night.

I was really picky about what kind of stuff the doctors sent to my house to change my dressing. One week they sent these weird dressings that didn't stick very well. They wrapped too big around my arm and weren't comfortable. Another week they changed the kind of anti-bacterial scrubby the nurse used to disinfect the skin where my PICC line went into my body. The new one hurt way worse than the other one had. Using solvent to help remove the dressing was not good. The solvent made my skin develop a painful rash. And if my skin wasn't completely dry before a new dressing was put on it, then my skin would get a burn.

I paid really careful attention every time a nurse changed my dressing and made sure to use the kinds of dressings and scrubbies I preferred, and that my skin was dry and that they didn't use solvent. It hurt bad enough to have the dressing pulled off my skin without having rashes or burns to deal with. The nurses didn't usually work with kids, and the infusion specialists and home healthcare nurses weren't used to having a kid on a PICC line for so long. They seemed happy to learn from me what worked and what didn't.

I didn't feel like I knew my friends any more. I only showed up for one class then went straight home. Besides, why would my friends want to come hang out with me? All I could do was lay on the couch. They were all getting excited about skiing, and they went to dances at the school. I didn't even remember what my friends looked like and I didn't know what they thought was fun or cool any more. I didn't know what was worse, living with *Burnie* every day or laying on a couch hooked up to an IV all night and most of the day.

The only thing that was good was that I started being able to drink more Gatorade and I tried eating some animal crackers. And I didn't throw them up. The nutritionist said I could start trying to eat a little bit at a time. She said I didn't need to worry about hurting anything. If I ate something my body wouldn't tolerate, I would just throw it back up. Great.

Mom

Slowly Kevin started sipping more Gatorade. He even began to take some bites of animal crackers. Then he asked me to get him a slice of turkey. This confused me. Before the surgery Kevin survived on donuts and protein shakes we made with fruit. Three months after the surgery Kevin asked for deep fried chicken. He could only eat a few bites before the meat made him feel squeamish, but still -- the rapid shift from sugary food to deep fried meat was stark. I asked our nutritionist what she thought of this shift. She thought perhaps it would be better for Kevin to focus on foods that were easier to digest but said not to worry, something to eat was better than nothing to eat.

Once a week I had a scheduled call with a nutritionist. The nutritionist reviewed Kevin's blood work, weight gain, and eventually his food intake. With this information she would send a prescription off to our pharmacist who made the individually prepared TPN mixture for Kevin. This TPN would be delivered to our house twice a week.

TPN costs $556.00 a serving. At this price, I was happy to encourage turkey or fried chicken.

Kevin

I knew I was getting better. First, Katie made me a PVC pipe AK47 that I could load with marshmallows to shoot at her and Phillip. Of course, Phillip was a better shot than me, so I got pummeled with marshmallows. Then I started wanting to eat a little bit of food. I had started drinking some Gatorade, but the food was a bigger deal. I have no idea why I wanted turkey and deep-fried chicken, but that's what sounded good to me.

The funny thing is, the nurse who came to visit each week to torture me with a dressing change thought that maybe I should first eat baby food.

What? I thought. *This picture is warped.*

But my Mom went to the store and bought one of each kind of Stage 3 Gerber baby foods.

Seriously.

Okay, so there are some that don't sound too bad. Like plum applesauce. There are others that I don't think they should even feed to babies, like ground-up veal.

Here I am, nearly 15 years old and my mom was opening all of these different jars of baby food, trying to get me to take bites.

At least she didn't act like the spoon was an airplane coming in for a landing in my mouth.

No way was I eating the baby food, though. I wanted chicken.

When we went to see Dr. Downey and I told him about wanting to eat fried chicken and not baby food, he smiled. Not like I had told a funny joke, but an "Oh, isn't that interesting" smile.

Then he told me that fried chicken is really slow to digest. Maybe the reason that I wanted fried chicken is because then my intestines wouldn't have to work so hard or so fast or something. He seemed to think that it was really cool that when I was growing up and before my surgery I would eat little tiny bits of sugary, fast-digesting foods, and now that my intestines wouldn't work I wanted to eat little bits of really slow-digesting food. He said something about how everyone should listen so well to what their bodies were telling them to eat.

That made me feel good. And so did the fried chicken.

Mom

Three months had passed since Kevin's surgery. Kevin's ability to tolerate bites of chicken and turkey were encouraging. He could drink Gatorade. He took fewer pain pills and less anti-nausea medicine. Progress was slow, but it was progress, and we all hung on to each little step forward.

Kevin

The coolest night that I remember was the night of the Presidential elections.

I got to see Barack Obama in person a long time ago, before I got sick. He talked to a couple hundred of us that showed up at this corner when he was just deciding to run for President.

I had never heard a politician speak before, but this guy was cool. He talked about how he wanted kids to be educated and how he wanted everyone to have healthcare. He made some funny jokes about how his wife made him act.

Then in the hospital I would hear people cheering when he would talk about how important hope was and how we were ready for change. Yeah, I got that for sure. I hoped my stomach would stop hurting and I hoped that my life would change so I could be a normal kid.

Then after I got out of the hospital I would listen to this radio station that played the speeches of everyone running for office. Obama was still my favorite. He was always positive, and he didn't say mean things about other people, even when they were saying mean things about him. And mostly he kept going on about hope and, "Yes we can."

It reminded me some of what Coach Wooden had said, before I knew I was really sick, about believing in yourself and being respectful and working hard.

So that night when we were waiting to see who would be our next president, I wanted to go over to the Botkins' house to be around all of our neighbors who were cheering for Barack Obama.

This might not seem like a big deal for a lot of people, but to my mom this was huge. I hadn't gone to anyone's house since I got out of the hospital. I had tried to go to one soccer game, but that was really hard. I couldn't stand to smell things cooking and I was still too tired to be around crowds of people. But when we turned on the television to see who was winning, I wanted to walk over to our good friends' house and celebrate with them.

The group at the Botkins' house got real quiet when it was time for the last votes to come in that made Barack Obama president. Then everyone cheered and I liked *noise* for the first time in almost two years.

Mom came to sit next to me when President-elect Obama gave his acceptance speech. I peeked over at her while he was talking and she had tears running down her face. I think we were both thinking the same thing.

Sometimes hope wins.

CHAPTER TEN

The Power of Hope

(September 2008 – March 2009)

Kevin

Listening to Barack Obama's acceptance speech made me realize that I should keep hoping that my intestines would start working and that someday I would be able to play soccer and hang out with my friends again. Until then, I kept spending time at doctors' offices and getting better.

Dr. Downey said that the problem was with, as he put it, "the motility" of my intestines. Nearly three months after the surgery, my intestines still weren't working.

See, intestines are muscles. Mine had been stretched out so much because of the big-time blockage my arteries had caused. So my intestines weren't strong enough to contract the way muscles should if they are going to work right.

What we didn't know for the longest time is if they had been stretched out for so long that they had become atrophic, which would mean that they would never work again. If they had become atrophic then I guess I would have had to live the rest of my life on a surgically implanted feeding tube.

The other problem that I knew about was that people could really only live on TPN for about eight months. The reason they checked my blood levels every week was to make sure that my liver was still working. If you live on TPN for too long then your liver gets all huffy and quits working because it thinks you don't need it any more. So from the time that I had my surgery in March until Christmas Eve, we had no idea if my intestines were ever going to work again.

Before my Christmas Eve appointment with Dr. Downey, it felt like they never would work again. We started a new routine in our house where Mom would get up at three a.m. to hook up the IV so I could get better sleep. My PICC line kept me from getting good sleep. We all thought that I would be done with it soon, so I kept toughing it out.

Finally, we decided to split up the hours that it would run, so that I could sleep at night. I would take a sleeping pill and once that made me fall sound asleep, my mom would wake up and come in to start the pump. I started feeling a lot better once I was getting more sleep.

I was putting on some serious weight too. I slowly started snacking more during the day. All those calories, plus my TPN, helped me get to over 90 pounds. This was a huge deal for me since I was getting close to getting my learner's permit and I really didn't want to have to have to use a booster seat when I was learning how to drive.

Still, the whole PICC line and not knowing if my intestines would ever work again pretty much stunk. The TPN made me cold and clammy. Plus, sometimes Phillip would forget that I had the PICC line in my arm so he would whack me like a normal brother would – right on the PICC insertion. That would really hurt.

And my guts still really hurt. It felt like people were having a tug of war inside me. I wished so bad those little people pulling on my insides would get a life.

It was weird to think about, but I didn't really remember my first five years of life, so I only remembered the last ten. Of those ten I had been in pain and nauseated for a year and a half. Anyway, basically about 15 percent of my life I had been in pain and nauseated. And the rest of the time I couldn't eat. Crazy.

And crazy that after not going to school for almost two years, I could still do math to figure all of that out.

Mom

All Kevin wanted for Christmas was to have his PICC line removed. That did not happen. What we did get for Christmas was Dr. Downey's conviction that there was ample indication that Kevin's duodenum functionality was increasing, signaling an eventual restoration to the damaged muscle. The other gift Dr. Downey gave to Kevin was an approval to cut down to eight hours of TPN a day.

Eight hours instead of 12 hooked up to an IV was life altering. Kevin continued to slowly gain weight as he was able to consume more calories on his own. His reliance on the PICC line to provide his nutrition would slowly diminish as his food intake increased. The first decrease in TPN signaled hope that other changes were soon to come. The less time Kevin spent tied to an IV, the more energy he gained. He began to visit friends. My heart leapt into my throat the first time Phillip and Kevin began to wrestle. I interrupted as a referee, checking that Kevin's IV port was securely protected under colorful bandages to avoid the risk of catching and pulling out the carefully placed catheter.

After a big snowstorm, I returned home from work to find Kevin and Katie playing with their snow skates on jumps they had built in our back yard. With no prompting from me, Kevin had ventured out into the snow to play with his sister. It was a normal winter scene that held super-normal meaning for me.

But soon, we would share an opportunity that was far from normal. An opportunity that took us further down the path of healing and hope.

Kevin

It seemed like a cool idea at first.

As soon as Barack Obama was elected to be the next president of the United States, our friends in Annapolis, the Flaglers, called and said we should come out for the Inauguration. Mom and Dad talked about it, and before I knew it, Dad had bought the airline tickets, and Mom was trying to get tickets to the Inauguration.

Dad said that so many people were going out for the Inauguration that we couldn't fly into Washington DC. Instead we were going to fly into New York and catch the train down to stay with the Flaglers. Then we would go with them from their house into the city to watch Obama being sworn in as President.

There were all kinds of issues to deal with, though. First, everyone in the world wanted to be at the Inauguration, so getting tickets was impossible. Then, I was still living on TPN, so I had to travel with liquids, a pump, all my medicine and a wheelchair. On top of everything, we had to fly out on my birthday, so I couldn't get my driver's permit when I wanted to.

But mostly, I was kind of worried about how much energy it was going to take to travel clear across the country in the middle of winter. We would be in the middle of a crowd of millions of people. At first I got excited about the idea, so my parents put the plan into action. After they did, I got afraid of what I had gotten myself into!

Mom

Traveling to the Inauguration began as a joke between Jeff and me. Our friends called from back east and said we should come on out, they had a place for us to stay. We thought about the message of hope and how it had carried us through the past couple of months. On a whim, Jeff got online and looked at airline tickets. Not even a day after Obama had won the election, flights into Washington DC were already full. Tickets to New York were still available and priced low. We had to make a decision right then.

We needed accommodations in New York City, and we would be walking on air if we could get tickets to the Inauguration. Worst case, we decided, we would go hang out at the National Mall with a million of our "closest friends." Of course, we really wanted tickets. So did everyone in the United States.

I began my campaign to secure tickets. I wrote e-mails that very next day to every Utah Senator and Representative. Newspaper articles the same day reported overloaded e-mail systems throughout politicians' inboxes as millions of ordinary citizens like myself requested tickets.

Representative Bishop quickly replied with a formal letter. He had 200 tickets available to him and they were already taken. A kind e-mail response came from Senator Hatch. There would be no tickets available from his 400-ticket allotment, but we were welcome to join in a Senator's reception in the Hart Building after the Inauguration. In fact, Senator Hatch's thoughtful receptionist told me of prior Inaugurations, the cold, the standing, and the waiting. She thought that with Kevin so ill, we might be better off just watching the Inauguration from inside the warmth of the reception room.

Representative Matheson, the only Democrat representing the

state of Utah, was inundated with requests. His e-mail box was full. My request never got through.

After two weeks we figured we would be joining the masses without tickets that were to be descending on the city. Even if we were to stand out on the National Mall without tickets, the idea of participating first hand in the celebration of Obama's unlikely Presidential election seemed worth the effort. The tie-in with Kevin's health battle was that strong.

Just before Christmas, an e-mail from Senator Bennett's office popped up in my inbox. "Could you please contact our office; we have four tickets set aside for your family." The office needed confirmation that we would use them.

I had written a brief summary of the motivation and hope Kevin had gained by following the election. The staff at Senator Bennett's office felt that Kevin's struggle was worthy of tickets. But four tickets was their absolute limit. The demand was too great to extend to even one more individual.

Jeff convinced himself that he would be content to mill with the crowds filling up the National Mall outside the ticketed area.

We were all so excited! What an opportunity this would be!

The time to travel for the Inauguration drew near. Kevin's intestines refused to heal. Our trip would be confounded with TPN, pumps, wheelchairs, medicines, and Kevin still too weak to handle an aggressive travel schedule. I contacted a friend who had connections at the Marriott Hotel. Kevin would need a place to rest, a refrigerator to store his medicine and TPN, a room where he could run his pump without interfering with everyone's sleep. Everything fell into place. Thanks to my friend's persuasion, the Marriott graciously provided a multi-room suite with a refrigerator right in the heart of Times Square.

Touched by all of the events that had transpired making it possible for us to have a front row seat for this historic event, I wrote an editorial to our local newspaper titled: "What the Inauguration Means to Me." Our local radio station picked up the editorial. I was interviewed, and mentioned our exciting news; we had four tickets to the Inauguration. The reporter noted that there were five people in our family.

Within minutes of the radio interview broadcast, our phone rang. Old soccer friends of ours had a son serving in the Navy who had an extra ticket. We now had a ticket for everyone.

Kevin

The worst birthday ever.

I turned fifteen and should have been going to get my driver's permit and getting together with my friends. Instead I was woken up at 5:30 a.m. It would take us forever to get my PICC line turned off, all the really warm clothes set for a trip to the sub-arctic east coast, then all of my medical stuff loaded up and cleared through security at the airport.

All of us kids were tired, and Mom and Dad were stressed out. Trying to fly with a sick kid is hard. There were special forms that the doctor had to write, special appointments with doctors to make sure I would be okay, special times to meet with the nurses that changed my central line dressing, special packing to keep my TPN and medicine cold, and special forms to let us carry all of my liquid food and medicine on board the flight. And I was cold. And nauseated. But the very worst part? We got all the way to New York City, checked into our hotel and went to find someplace to eat dinner before anyone remembered that it was my birthday.

Everybody in the world was excited because a plane had made an emergency landing in the Hudson River, just right up the street from where we were staying in New York City. Everyone on the plane had lived. Everywhere we went people called it a miracle and told us we could walk up the street to see the plane for ourselves in the morning.

And everywhere we went in the airport and in the taxi and along the streets, there were Obama t-shirts, buttons and hats. No one realized that I thought it was a big deal that I had turned 15.

To be honest, I had told my parents that I didn't want a party. Or even any friends coming over. And there wasn't a birthday cake or anything that I would even be able to eat. Mom and Dad had made a big deal out of me opening my cards from my uncles, aunts, cousins and grandparents, and had put streamers up in the kitchen the weekend before we left. They had told me that they wanted to do something special for me when we were in New York -- like go to a Broadway play or something.

Finally Mom asked if I was feeling all right. I think she was afraid the travel to New York had been too hard on me, and it had been hard, but that wasn't what was wrong.

"No one remembered my birthday," I told her.

Oh, man, then she felt awful. She must have told Dad because both of them did everything they could to make it up to me. But there was nothing I wanted except to be able to eat like a normal person and not be so tired and cold all the time and not have these two guys living in my gut playing tug-of-war with my intestines.

I did use their forgetting my birthday to my advantage a little bit. When my brother, sister and I wanted extra keepsakes, I mentioned my birthday, and my parents could hardly refuse.

Mom

After a couple of days to adjust to the new time zone and settle Kevin down a bit, we caught the train down to DC. We were on a tight timetable. The tickets to the Inauguration had to be picked up by the people whose names were listed on them during a window 24 – 48 hours prior to the Swearing-in Ceremony.

There were all kinds of measures in place to make certain no one bought or cheated their way into the event. And we needed to get Jeff's ticket. With over 100,000 tickets issued, the odds that Jeff's ticket would be near to those provided by Senator Hatch's office were slim. We would most likely be far from each other and would have to make arrangements to meet after the huge event.

What were the odds of Jeff's seat being right with ours? But it was. We were all in the front portion of the yellow section. All that was left was figuring out how we were going to get into the city and through the security lines in time for the start of the Inauguration. Over a million people were making the same commute.

Our friends, the Flaglers, had been working on the logistics for weeks. They had researched alternatives, conducted a practice run and figured out that our best bet was to drive further out of the city to the starting point of the bus routes. This way there would be somewhere to park the cars and, as this was the terminus location, get seats on the bus. The bus would bring us to the end point of the subway that would carry us into the mall. But we would need to make an early start.

The bus portion was genius. We were early enough that we had to wait only three busloads before it was our turn to board. Once on the bus we could relax for the 45-minute ride over an interstate closed to all but authorized vehicles. A mile out from the Metro we realized the cleverness of our friends. Cars were parked illegally along the side of the freeway. People were walking miles from every direction. The parking lots were full and overloaded. The crowds of people made me think of Orson Welles' *War of the Worlds* -- tens of thousands of people crushing their way forward, pushing their way to get on the trains headed into the city.

Fortunately for us, we had Metro tickets in hand and a wheelchair. A policeman found us waiting in line, noted Kevin bundled in the wheelchair and asked us to follow him. He brought us to a special entrance with an elevator that led straight up to the platform. We rolled onto the next train, which should have delivered us to the National Mall in 22 minutes. Before we reached the third stop from our destination, the train came to a halt. Sitting in the dark tunnel, we were informed that the crowds were too dense on the National Mall; people were unable to make their way off the train and up to the street level. We were trapped down below.

Kevin slept comfortably in his wheelchair. An hour passed. Jeff and I were aware that we still had a long walk behind the Capital where we were to join in another line to clear security. But the joy of the day was not to be dampened. People on the train began to get to know one another, cheering for a variety of reasons. Our home state of Utah got a special "Utah in the house" cheer. Behind us sat a statesman from Canada who would be joining the Presidential party up on the risers. Across from us was a 104-year-old woman, a daughter of slaves, whose eyes filled with tears at the significance of the day.

Trapped beneath the Washington streets, faced with the risk of missing the entire Inauguration, the mood in the train car was still jubilant. Not a single person grumbled, not an ill word was spoken.

Half an hour later we heard an announcement. The train would be terminating three stops early. The crowds were too thick and moving too slowly for the train to make it any further. Jeff pulled out our maps to figure out a new plan for making it around the capital and to the security check-in point in time to see the swearing-in of the 44th President of the United States of America. Timing would be tight he informed me. We had a long walk ahead of us, pushing Kevin's wheelchair.

As we prepared to depart the stalled train another announcement was made. Tracks had cleared. The next stop would bring us to our original destination. We might just be able to make it to our seats in time. The train inched forward to our preferred stop, opened the doors and we were faced with a sea of people. We joined the throng of people moving inches at a time, all slowly, patiently making our way to see Barack Obama sworn in as the 44th President.

Saying good-bye to the Flaglers, after making plans to regroup at the end of the ceremony, we headed to our special security check-in point. Once again, Kevin's wheelchair granted us special access to a shorter security line, then on up to a designated seating area for wheelchair bound individuals. Right on the steps of the Capitol.

Kevin

When we got on the train, I told everyone in my family they needed to thank me. No way we would have made it on the train without my wheelchair pass. I guess without my wheelchair, there's no way my family and I would have even gotten to be part of the Inauguration either, so fair's fair.

We stood in line for security, and Mom and Dad pushed me up to where we would be sitting for the Inauguration. Then I was really glad that I had my chair. There was a special handicap section right in front of the podium where they were going to swear-in the President. We didn't need binoculars or a big screen or anything to see everything going on. The military band was playing, kids' choirs were singing and famous people kept walking by us.

Man, though, I was cold.

Finally the cold got so bad, I begged Mom to come with me early to the Senator's reception where we could watch the President get sworn in from inside a warm building on a big screen TV. No way was she leaving, though.

Instead she took off her coat, wrapped it around me, got out more hand warmers and stuck them inside my coat and told me that someday I would thank her for making me stay. All of you probably watched the Inauguration, so you know that she was right.

Hearing Obama's speech and seeing his strength gave me strength to continue my healing. I was really glad that my parents forced me to stick it out for the trip and through the speech.

Mom

As difficult as the journey was, it was absolutely worth it. Our trip served as a reminder of the power of strength and understanding and compassion.

Through Kevin's long-suffering eyes, we were able to look to President Barack Obama's Inauguration as a signal of the strengthening of compassion and understanding, and the power of *Hope.*

For 18 months we had fought for Kevin's health. There were times when the future looked bleak. Just as the country and world needed to pull together against unfathomable national challenges, our family, friends and community had pulled together against

Kevin's difficult health situation to bring a brighter future into our home.

When we had gathered as a family nearly two years earlier to hear Senator Obama talk to a sparse crowd in a parking lot in Utah, we had no idea of how strongly his message of hope would carry our family through the health, education, and financial trials we were to face. The powerful message our family heard on that summer day in 2007 would echo deeply a year later as Kevin lay in the hospital, heavily sedated from a life saving surgery, while strains of the convention speeches filtered in over the beep-beep of the heart monitor.

We drew strength from a leader bringing to life a message of compassion and understanding, the message of hope and change.

Throughout Kevin's pain and suffering, Senator Obama's speeches became our own personal message of hope and change. During the long road to recovery, the nation mirrored our family's story.

The election campaign focused on education. We were reminded of this as teachers came to the hospital to cheer on Kevin's recovery. The teachers donated their spare time acting as tutors to enable him to join his high school buddies back in the classroom.

Debates about healthcare issues became deeply personal. I struggled to maintain my job so that our healthcare did not lapse. We saw children in hospital rooms spend their days alone so that their parents could work. This resonated with my own exhaustion and heartache. I grew to realize the healthcare challenges faced by parents of ill children.

The economy melted, and so did our family's financial resources. A loan promised from a bank for Jeff's small business evaporated along with our savings. On top of the worry of a child's health, we had to worry about how we would pay our bills, and if we would be able to send Phillip to college.

These were dark days for us, yet Barack Obama believed in hope, and he reminded us that we should, too.

Kevin

It was a long road to get to play high school soccer in the spring, but I made it.

Mom

As we watched from the sidelines in what seemed like slow motion, we all saw Kevin connect with the soccer ball for a glorious one-touch goal. From 20 yards out, the ball sailed straight into the top right corner of the net!

Five months after Obama was elected and three months after we had travelled to Washington DC to be part of the historic inauguration, Kevin brought his '*A game*' to the soccer field. Nearly eight months after his surgery, Kevin felt up to attending school every other day.

On game day Kevin had already pushed himself to his max. He rose at 6:30 a.m., went to four classes then headed over to the field for warm-ups with the high school soccer team. The weather was bone-chilling, snow-blowing cold out on the field.

Coach Paul had worked with Kevin throughout the season, and figured out that Kevin could, on average, handle about three minutes of play before his strength would give out. Much to Kevin's joy, he consistently gave my son that chance.

Kevin hadn't been in the game for more than fifteen seconds when a pass was crossed to him from 25 yards out. Kevin connected with such strength behind the kick, the ball flew into the back of the net.

Everyone on the field stopped in their tracks, and then his team erupted in cheers, wrapping Kevin in hugs of congratulations. The parents watching the game stood – stunned, tears in their eyes.

The significance of the moment was lost on no one, with the exception of the opposing team. They must have thought it quite strange that a bunch of high school boys stopped to hug one player after their team scored its third straight goal.

The goal confirmed to Kevin so many things: his strength, his tenacity, and his survival. It helped him to believe he would make a full recovery, and it reminded him of the support that surrounded him.

His *Facebook* message that day claimed that he hadn't known he had the strength to kick the ball that far. But he rose a bit earlier each morning and ate a bit more food each day. He led the charge to the ski area where we skied together as a family for the first time in two years. He offered to help Jeff cook with garlic and onions for Easter dinner and the smells didn't drive him out of the kitchen. He stayed at the table for the meal, and then afterwards, the egg coloring and egg smashing. He even hopped onto his skateboard to join us all for a walk after the meal.

And he began smiling more.

Obama's message of hope brought us to the final phases of healing. And that hope gave Kevin the strength to shoot that soccer ball into the back of the net.

CONCLUSION

Life Without Burnie

(March 2009 – September 2009)

Kevin

I still had a lot of healing to do. The month before Dr. Downey took my central line out was maybe the longest month of my short 15 years. At the end of February, I got to try not hooking up to TPN to see how I did just by eating. I lost three pounds and my labs came back not looking too good, so I had to go back on TPN. Yuck.

Then I got a bad virus, and that didn't help me. I lost more weight and didn't want to eat. At least I still had Zofran and Reglan to take so I didn't throw up.

By the end of March I was really upset. The adhesions from my surgery hurt. My PICC line hurt. I hated getting my dressing changed. When my favorite home healthcare nurse came to change my dressing, I didn't talk to her; I wouldn't even look at her.

Mom once gave me 97 seconds to feel sorry for myself. I cried. I asked her, "Why me?"

I told her that if the doctors had figured out what was wrong with me the first time I went into the hospital then I could be playing soccer and feeling like I was really part of the team, not still stuck with a central line to feed me and pain in my gut and in my arm and even in my legs when I got growing pains.

I told her I couldn't take it anymore. I was tired of having to "be strong." I was tired of "rallying." I was tired of looking at my situation from the bright side, you know, "alive and getting better." I just wanted to be like all of my friends. Since she only gave me 97 seconds, I had a lot of feeling sorry for myself to fit in there.

And then, a week later when I went in for my monthly check up with Dr. Downey, *he took it out.* Just like that, he pulled out my PICC line really fast, before I even knew what was happening.

It was really weird not to have the port swinging out under my arm at first -- in a good way. I was most excited about not having to cover it up to take a shower. I could finally get into a hot tub or go swimming with my friends. After almost eight months, I was mostly glad that I didn't have to wrap up my arm just to play soccer.

My Mom said that she was most glad not to worry about watching me in pain when I got my dressing changed or not getting an infection in my heart or air in the line or the line getting plugged or serious stuff like that. I guess she had a point, too.

It was really cool that we could all worry less and have less hassle. Dr. Downey told me that it would be maybe three more months and the pulling in my stomach should go away and I would be better than ever.

Mom

The policeman pulled me over and informed me that he had to impound my car. I looked confidently at him and said, "You really don't want to do that."

I went on to explain that my son was ill and had called. He urgently needed me to pick him up from school. Without a car, my child would be stranded.

Apparently the registration on the Honda had elapsed. The

tags were nearly seven months overdue. I didn't have the energy to explain to the officer what had transpired over the past seven months that took precedence over renewing car tags. I merely reiterated the fact that impounding the car was not a good idea. The young man in uniform verified my safe driving record, secured a promise that I would report to the DMV and register the car, and sent me on to pick up Kevin from school.

After settling Kevin back at home, I did as I was told. I updated my license plates, paid my back taxes, then secured the sticky new tags to my dusty license plates. And so it was with surprise that I opened up an official looking notice that contained a warrant for my arrest three months after the policeman had stopped me.

Kevin

It seemed weird to drive my Mom to the jail.

She made me drive her there so she could clear up the warrant for her arrest. I had just gotten my driver's permit, so I was willing to drive her practically anywhere.

I guess Mom had let some things slide while I was sick. One of the things was renewing the car's license registration. Another thing was clearing up the ticket she received for driving with expired tags. I hope this is the only time I see what a warrant for a person's arrest looks like. Still, I think it will always be a funny story to tell people that I drove my mom to jail when she got arrested, even if the story sounds a lot more serious than what really happened.

Mom

Looking back on the ordeal, it shouldn't have surprised me that I had overlooked paying my traffic ticket. There were so many parts of my life that I had ignored for so long. By June, each week brought a new onslaught of overdue bills, unpaid tickets, unanswered correspondence, and neglected relationships.

Kevin no longer had his PICC line for support, and I finally had time to clear up the accumulated fallout from two years of distress. The warrant for my arrest was the most pressing, but certainly not the most difficult to address.

Paying overdue doctor bills was harder emotionally than I could have imagined. Insurance companies dragged their feet on many charges. Jeff handled the back and forth correspondence until it became clear that we were held responsible for certain charges. Some I happily paid. Others hurt.

As I sorted through the money we owed, I revisited procedures that led us further away from a proper diagnosis. I paid for hospital treatments that had put Kevin's life at risk. I wrote checks for medicines that, at best, hadn't worked, and some that had made him much worse. There didn't seem to be an alternative, however. I paid them all and the bill collectors stopped calling.

There was one final phone call that needed to be addressed. This was the call I saved for last.

Primary Children's Medical Center had been calling for months. The Risk Manager wanted to know if we could share our story with her. She wanted to know what needed to be done based on the poor outcome Kevin received in his earlier hospitalizations. I put off the call, telling her that until we knew Kevin could live without supplemental nutrition, I wasn't ready to talk.

Now Kevin's central line was removed, and I steeled myself to share our experience with those who had the power to make certain this happened to no other child.

I met with the Risk Manager and told my story. We cried.

She asked what I would like to do. Jeff and I had talked quite a bit about this. And so I let her know that we wanted to do whatever might help the hospital learn from our misfortune.

She worked to set up a meeting with the hospital CEO and the team of doctors that had been unable to diagnose Kevin's illness so many months before.

The meeting was difficult. Reliving the experiences was painful. Listening to the doctors' ideas of what could have been handled differently to create a faster resolution to Kevin's illness hurt. Knowing that processes in the hospital had changed based on a case review helped. In the end, Jeff and I hoped that our story would continue to help the hospital improve.

There was a small degree of comfort knowing that the hospital no longer checked kids out of the hospital without strict psychiatric follow-up when a child was prescribed psychotropic medicines. Perhaps this could keep another family from a medically induced suicide watch, we hoped.

After this meeting, no great plans were put into place to help doctors work through conflict, or to encourage open communication, but the doctors who had been involved with Kevin's case saw the painful effects that a lack of teamwork could create. Perhaps hearing Kevin's story of pain caused by the inconsistent management of his care would encourage them to listen to one another, the nurses, the patients, and the caregivers in the future.

And new gastroenterologists had been hired. These new doctors could allow the over-burdened specialists to take more time with patients. Maybe with an eased patient-load, patients would not have to wait six months or be near death to be seen. Perhaps these doctors could spend more than their previous average of six minutes with each patient. More availability and more time, we hoped, would allow these specialists the ability to better diagnose complex medical conditions.

After the meeting, the Risk Manager wrote us a message thanking us for the effort and courage we had taken to share our side of Kevin's story with the doctors and the administration. She reaffirmed that lessons were learned by sharing our story, and that changes were already being made in hospital procedure based on Kevin's story and others like his. She let us know that we were welcome to meet again with the hospital administration.

The lessons I shared with the hospital administrators are the same lessons Kevin and I have shared throughout this book. Healthcare should center on the patient. Physicians need time, training and reinforcement to make sure they listen. A healthcare crisis requires a center caregiver to oversee the case and patient advocates to help navigate through the complex system. And, most importantly for our case, doctors need to let go of perceptual biases that lead them to diagnose and treat a horse when they hear hooves.

We didn't meet again. Instead, I sent the hospital administrators a letter that got me thinking about writing this book. The message talked about the lessons we had learned as we worked our way through the healthcare system. I told them what had enabled me to be the best possible healthcare advocate for Kevin. I mentioned calls I had been getting from other parents who were suffering from the same healthcare system limitations that had paralyzed our ability to get a proper diagnosis for Kevin.

I realize that hospital administrators are working to improve patient care through the channels they have available, but they need a story to help them understand the complexities and realities of a patient's experience. At the same time, someone needed to give hope to the parents and kids out there suffering from complex, chronic healthcare issues. Someone needed to offer a roadmap for healthcare advocacy. Someone needed to give patients and care givers inspiration and understanding when a cataclysmic health issue renders them hopeless. And so Kevin and I wrote this book.

During a low point in his recovery, Kevin mentioned how his misfortune could serve as a lesson for others someday. There were times when planning on making some good come out of all this bad was the motivation he needed to go through one more doctor appointment, one more procedure, one more painful dressing change.

And with that we turned our eyes to the future.

The warm summer days allowed Kevin a chance to try out his driving – even if it was to drive me to the jail to clear up my ticket. He had sleepovers and played. He swam and sat in hot tubs. He went to summer school and completed enough credits to advance to tenth grade. Together we wrote about his experience, in hopes that it might help someone else someday.

And I tried to remember how to sleep through the night.

I relearned how to do normal things. Picking up milk from the grocery store, taking the dog for a walk, sending birthday cards.

I'm still learning.

Kevin

I'm still a skinny kid – I shot up eight inches when I was 'eating' TPN. I weigh 100 pounds now. I didn't weigh enough or get strong enough to make the fall soccer league. I miss playing soccer. I miss seeing my friends during practice.

I did get third place in my Chinese class' *Simon Says* competition when school started again, though. Plus I'm starting to think about what I want to do in the future. There was an alcohol awareness day where we wore beer goggles to see how drinking affected our motor skills. I cracked my friends up when I declared that my new life goal was to "start the Beer Goggle Olympics."

And there isn't soccer every day, so I can get together with my buddies on the weekends. Plus I'm making new friends at the high school. There's this fun club at school called the *Elvish* club. We watch movies with elves in them, but mostly we use it as an excuse to hang out after school.

My friend posted a *Facebook* update on my page. It was a "Random fact about Kevin." He wrote, "Some say [Kevin] weighs less than .0005 pounds and as a child he was Eddie Murphy. Others say that when he turns sideways he is completely invisible, and his body is completely bare of hair." He also wrote, "Sorry, Kevin, we all love you still." I thought it was pretty funny. Someday they are all going to be jealous of me when we're old and I can eat whatever I want, but they have to worry about their weight.

The doctors think that my abdomen still hurts because I have adhesions. Or maybe I grew so tall, so fast after my surgery the new parts of my intestines got stretched and need time to adjust to my new height. I tried going to a physical therapist to see if that would help the pain go away, but it didn't help. I do go to a physical therapist who is helping me get better posture after years of hunching over the place that *Burnie* lived in my gut. And I still like to get massages since my muscles hurt when I try to make them work again.

If the little people who are playing tug-of-war inside my gut don't go away, my doctors promise they'll do something to make me feel better. There is no reason to live in constant pain, they say. I do my best to ignore the pain. It's not anywhere near as bad as *Burnie* was. When I'm busy at school or with my friends, I don't really think about the pulling that much.

Mom says she'll wait until I tell her I want to do something about the pulling; then, when I'm ready, we can go back to the doctors. There's no way I'm ready right now. I'm having too much fun hanging out with my friends, learning how to be a high school student and finally being able to eat whatever I want.

Mom

I lay in bed listening to my three teenagers get ready for school. It's only 6:30 and the morning is still dark. Katie's laugh fills the air after Kevin declares, "Sneak hug!"

In my mind I see Kevin's 5-foot-8 inch frame sneak up behind Katie in the semi-dark hall. She is distracted, loading up her backpack as he wraps his arms around her. Phil looks on, quiet but approving.

My mind drifts back to the day two years ago when I gave Kevin a desperate hug on that airplane, begging him to hold on through the pain.

A frightening image flashes through my brain. Jeff, fighting back tears as he holds Kevin tight, begs Kevin to hold on to life as he sinks further into his suicidal inclinations.

I think back to the hospital a year ago when Katie and Phillip, through tender hugs, each connect with Kevin, lying unconscious after his surgery.

And I celebrate this cheerful morning noise, knowing that *Burnie* is now gone.

AFTERWORD

(Spring 2011)

Kevin

Listening literally saved my life.

For a year and a half, I told doctors over and over again that the pain in my stomach was real. And not just everyday paper-cut pain, I'm talking extreme, intense pain.

I couldn't function, go to school or even eat. And instead of listening, the doctors completely ignored me, told me I was depressed and bulimic, and threw 10 prescriptions for anxiety and depression at me.

Obviously I wasn't depressed, so the anti-depressants made me depressed, and at times even suicidal. I was knocking at death's door for nearly 18 months.

Luckily, I had a few good listeners on my side, including my mom, my family and friends, and our family doctors. My mom listened and wasn't afraid to speak up for me when doctors ignored what I had to say.

My family and friends were listeners. They heard my pain and gave me hope when times got really tough. And, fortunately there were also doctors who listened, asked questions, and ran the necessary tests to figure out what was wrong.

I had a surgery that fixed the problem, and I am now recovering. I have gained 40 pounds and am on my way to being a normal teen.

Tribute

How do you thank an entire cast and crew, spread throughout the world for the care and support they provided over such a long road? Our family sat down to dinner one night to figure it out. Maybe a little gift, we mused.

Kevin knew exactly what he wanted to do. Kevin wanted to donate money back to Primary Children's Medical Center in honor of all of the people that had helped him get well – the doctors and nurses, his family and friends, the neighbors, colleagues and even perfect strangers who had kept him in their thoughts and prayers, who had made meals and sent packages, who had nurtured our bodies and souls, and who offered their well wishes.

He wanted us to write a check, and he wanted the check to go to the hospital's general fund, for Kevin was certain the hospital knew how best to spend the money. And he wanted to give the check to Dr. Downey because Dr. Downey represented all that was best about Kevin's hospital.

Acknowledgments

We have my mom, (Beverly Graham, known as Grammie to Kevin) and my dad (Reginald Graham, Papa) to thank for making this book possible. Grammie was the first person to encourage Kevin and me to commit our conversations to paper. On the days when it was too painful to relive the memories, Grammie would remind us that our story had the power to make a difference. Without her gentle prodding, along with her and Papa's early praise and painstaking editing, this book would not exist.

Jeff, Phillip and Katie were key players as well. The story printed on these pages is as much their story as it is Kevin's and mine. Katie was proud when her essay was included. Phil understood the importance of the story in context of the medical field he has chosen to pursue, and offered his blessing to have his part in our healthcare drama printed for the world to read. And then there is Jeff: father extraordinaire, caring husband, best friend. Jeff would have preferred to keep our family's experience quiet. Yet once it was clear that Kevin and I were determined to tell our story, Jeff became our biggest fan. This book is more than the story of Kevin's illness, it is the story of our family. Without the willingness of everyone in the family to share the story, our book would not exist.

As the book took shape and we began to search for a publisher, I was introduced to Kent Gustavson at Blooming Twig Books. Kent connected with our story immediately and brought a vision of a shared conversation to our writing. Thanks to him, Kevin's voice and mine mixed together to bring our story to life.

Our book is a story of community, caring and connection. As in any community, it is impossible to single out everyone who contributes to the overall outcome. And yet certain individuals provided contributions, edits, feedback and encouragement at just the right time in just the right way.

Kathleen Reardon is a longtime mentor and sage to both Kevin and me. Kathleen kept us connected to our project from the very beginning.

Marcia Clouser and Shelly Braun stepped in with meticulous edits at just the right time.

Shana Hopperstead and Kathleen Campana were steadfast in their encouragement and support.

Deena McCollough stood in our corner throughout the entire writing and publishing process. Deena kept us on track and reminded us of the importance of our message.

Thank you to everyone who has helped us on the journey toward Kevin's health, and thank you to those who helped this book become a reality.

Kevin and I thank you, the reader, as well. We hope that as you read our book, you were reminded that listening is a powerful tool that can be well used to change and even to save lives. Listen openly and attentively; dismiss biases and pre-conceived notions so that you can truly hear what is being said. Listen to those around you: family, friends, patients, and even strangers. Know that the act of listening can bring hope and encouragement to those around you.

- Vicki Whiting, July 2011

About the Authors

Kevin Whiting is entering his senior year of high school in Park City, Utah, where he lives with his family and his dog Cooie. He volunteers at a local hospital, hangs out with his friends, and works in a nearby clothing outlet. Kevin will participate in a Chinese exchange program prior to his high school graduation in the spring of 2012. After high school, Kevin plans to attend college to become a surgeon.

Vicki Whiting, PhD is a Professor of Management at the Gore School of Business at Westminster College in Salt Lake City, Utah. She also consults for numerous organizations throughout the country on leadership and executive development. Vicki loves to travel and has led groups of students and her family on trips across six continents. Vicki lives with her husband Jeff, and two of her three children, Kevin and Katie, in Park City, Utah. Her son Phillip is currently serving in the US Air Force Special Forces as a Pararescue Jumper.

For more information, to read about the remainder of the cast that made this book possible, and to explore links to websites the authors found useful as they fought for Kevin's health, please visit their website at: *vickiwhiting.com*